PETER'S LINE ALMANAC

volume one

BY PETER DELIGDISCH

Copyright 2016

ISBN: 978-1523838707

...and so on and soforth

Dedicated to anyone who
needs a little bit of
dedication and
motivation
of their own.

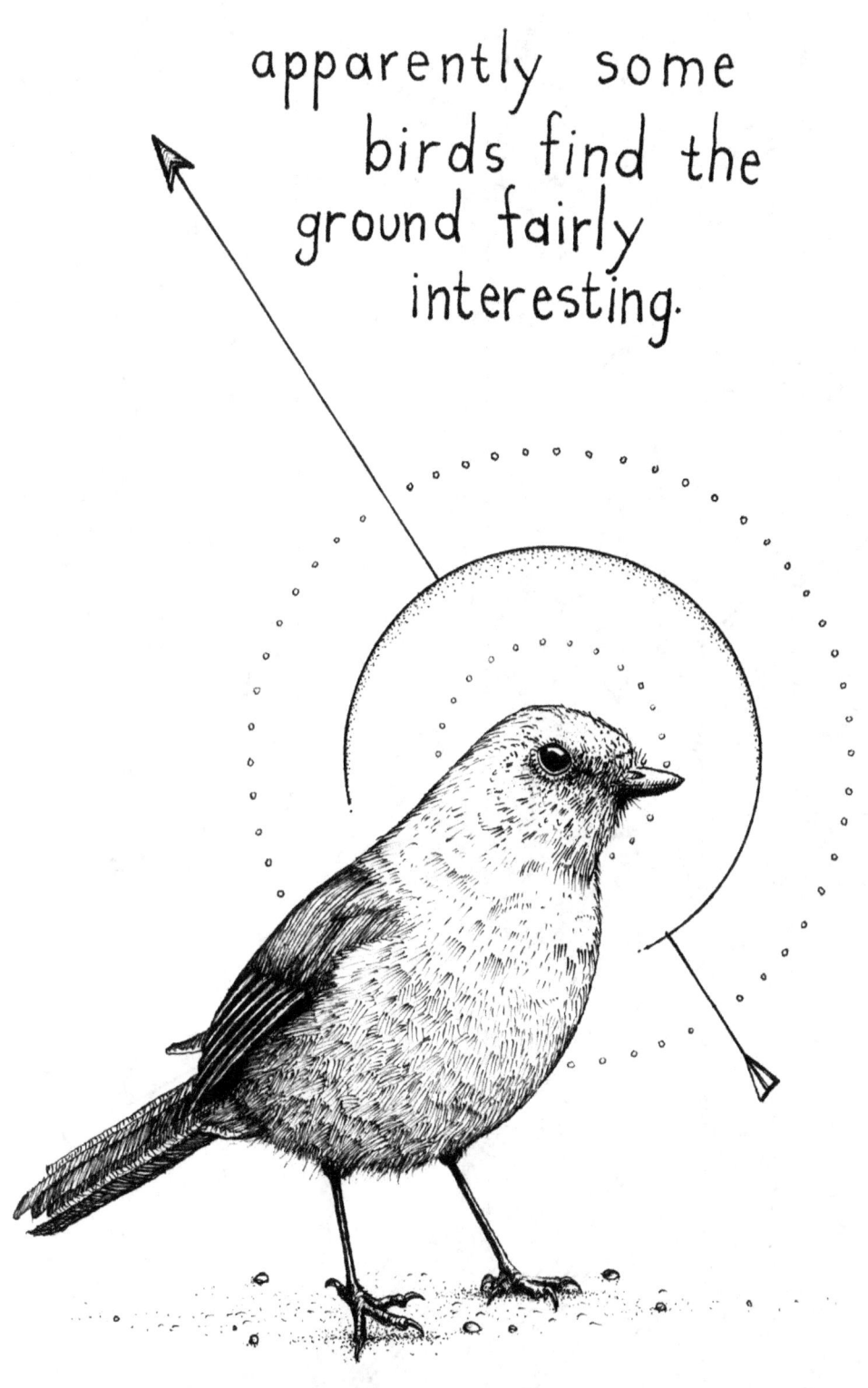

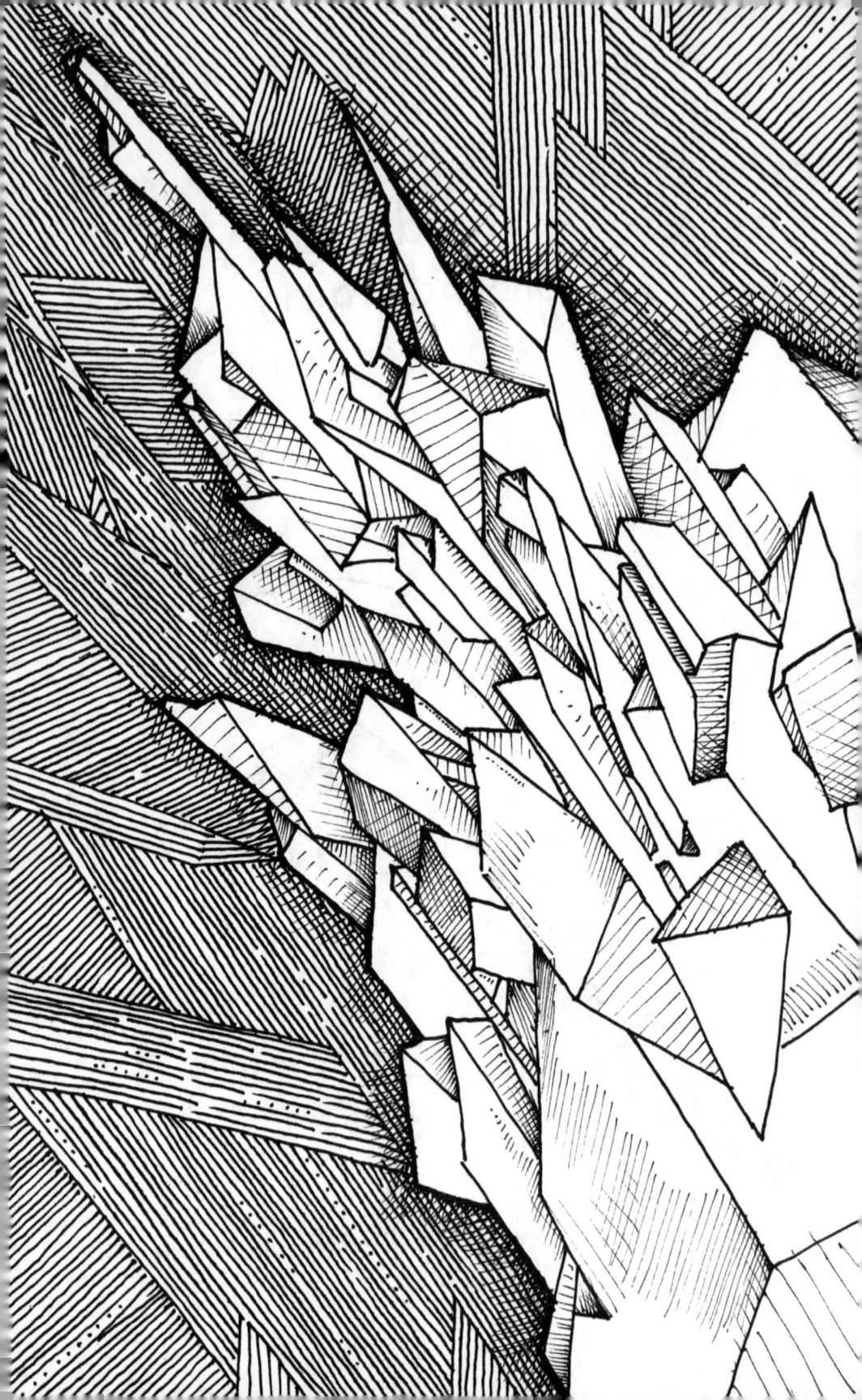

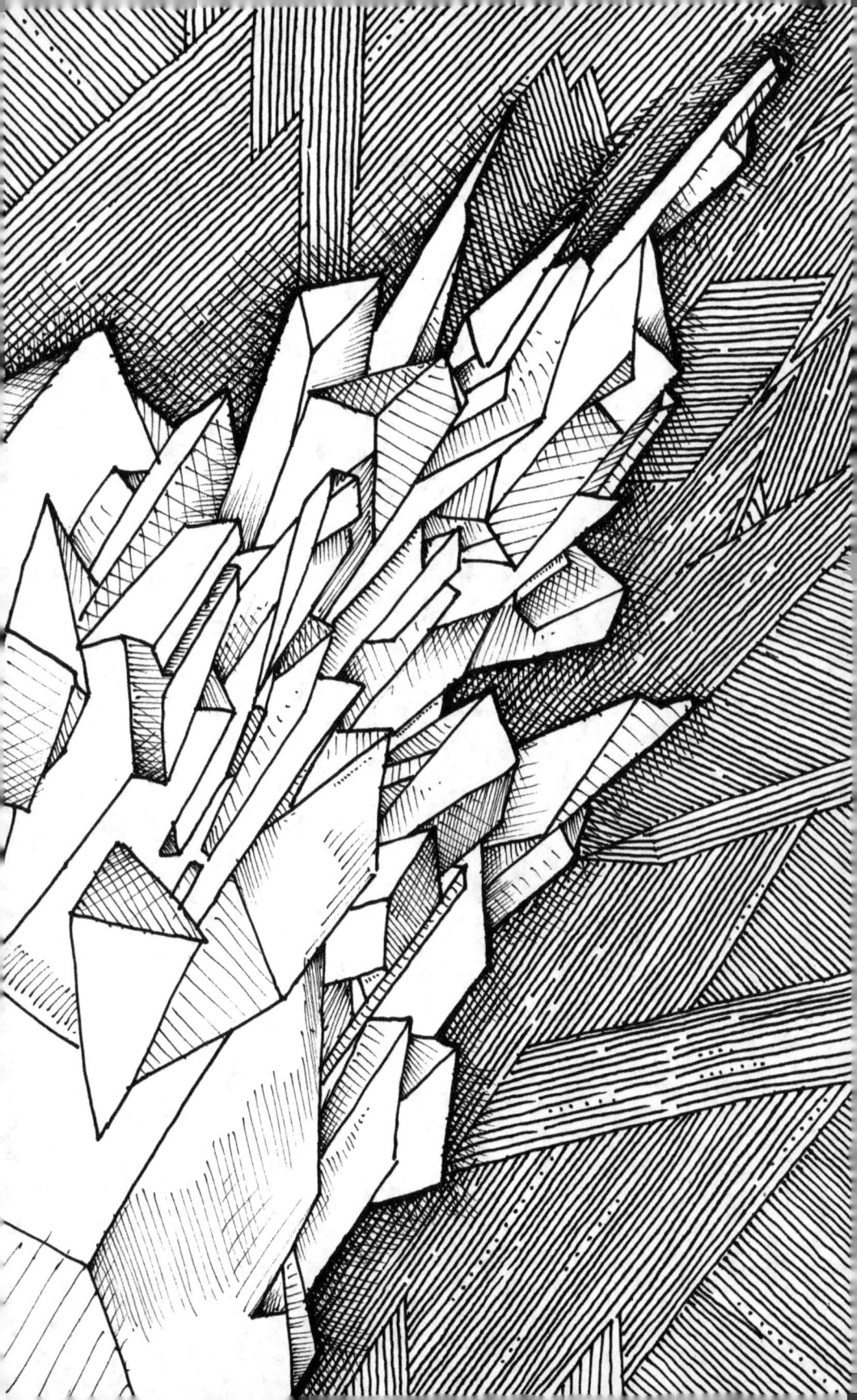

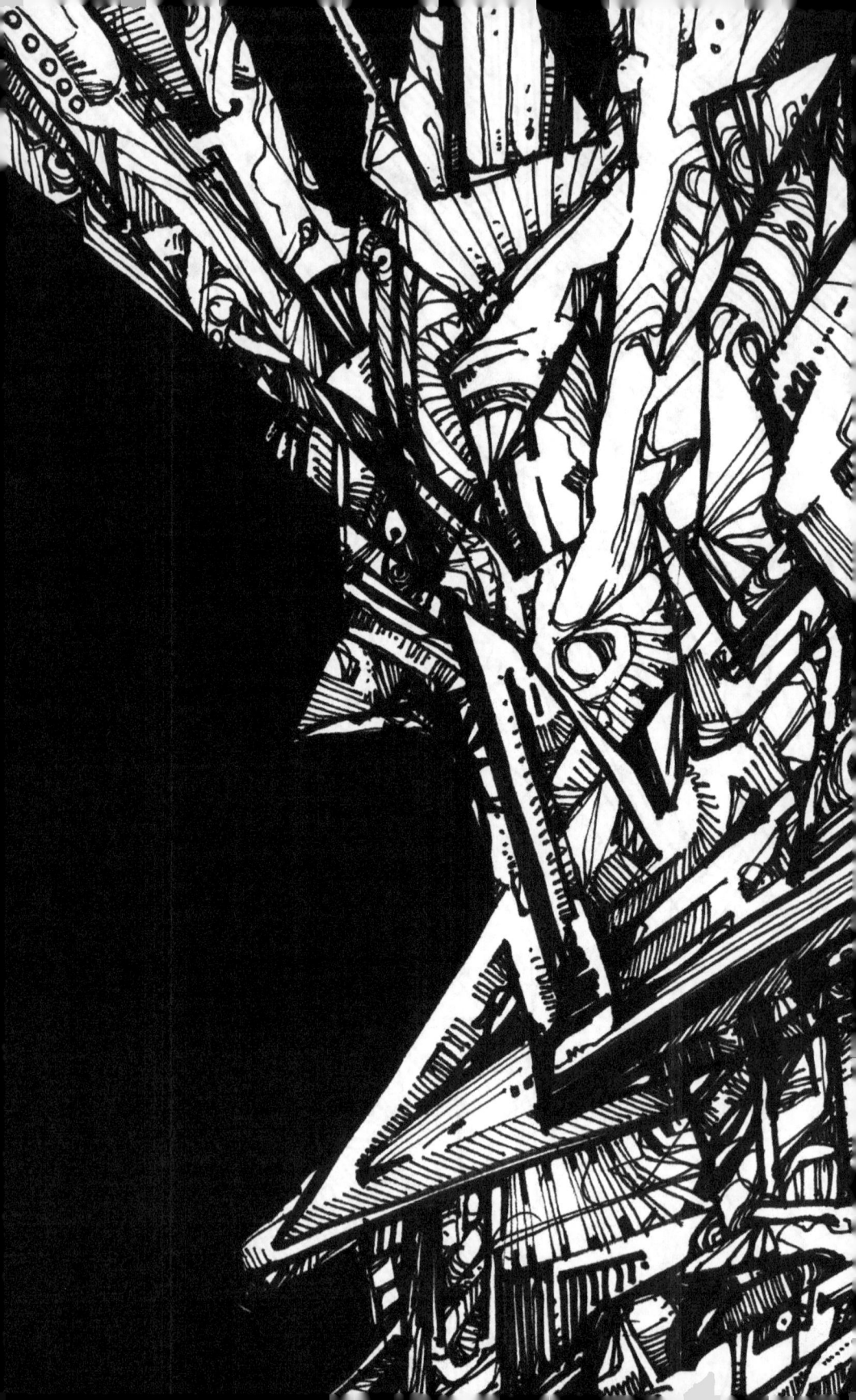

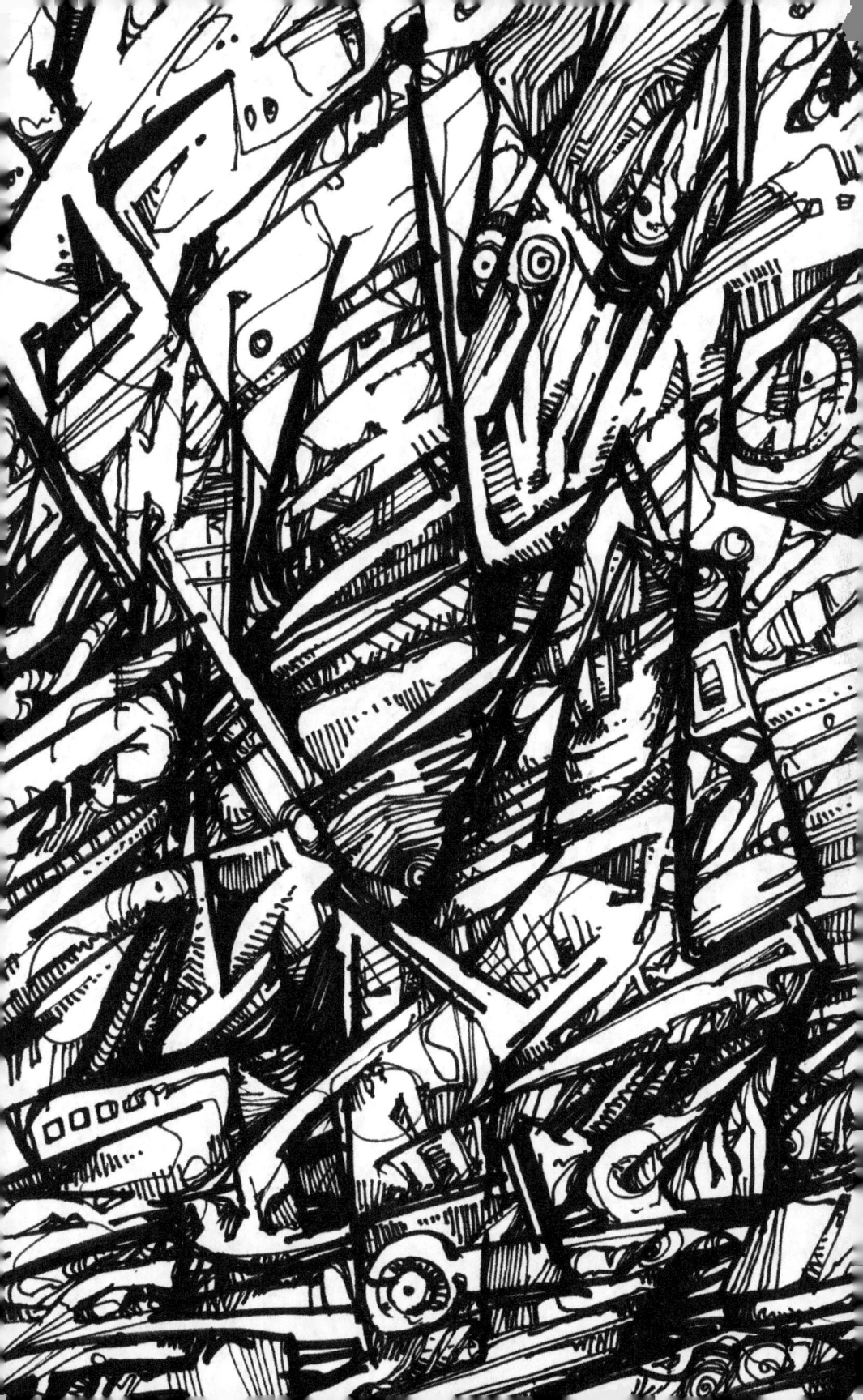

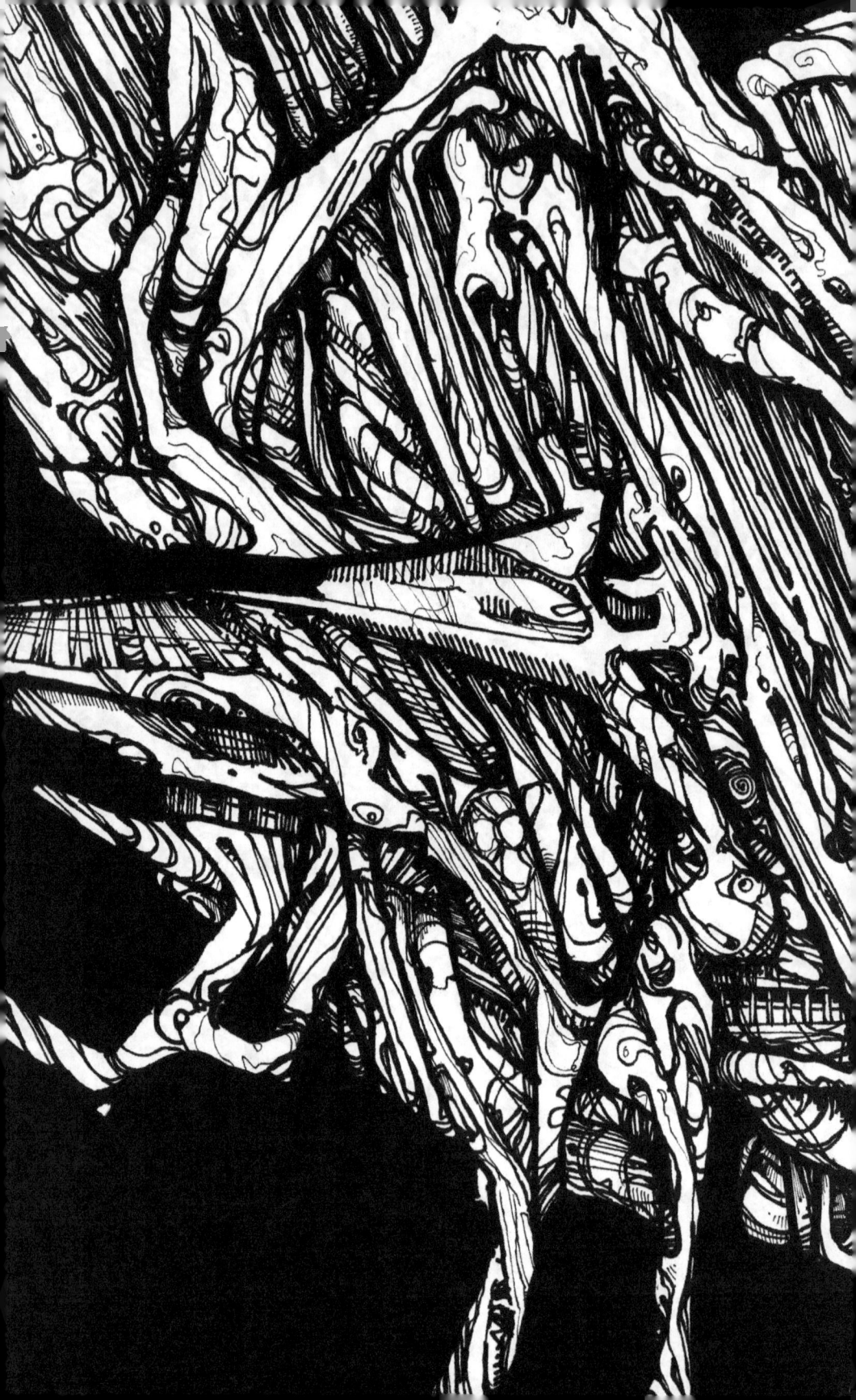

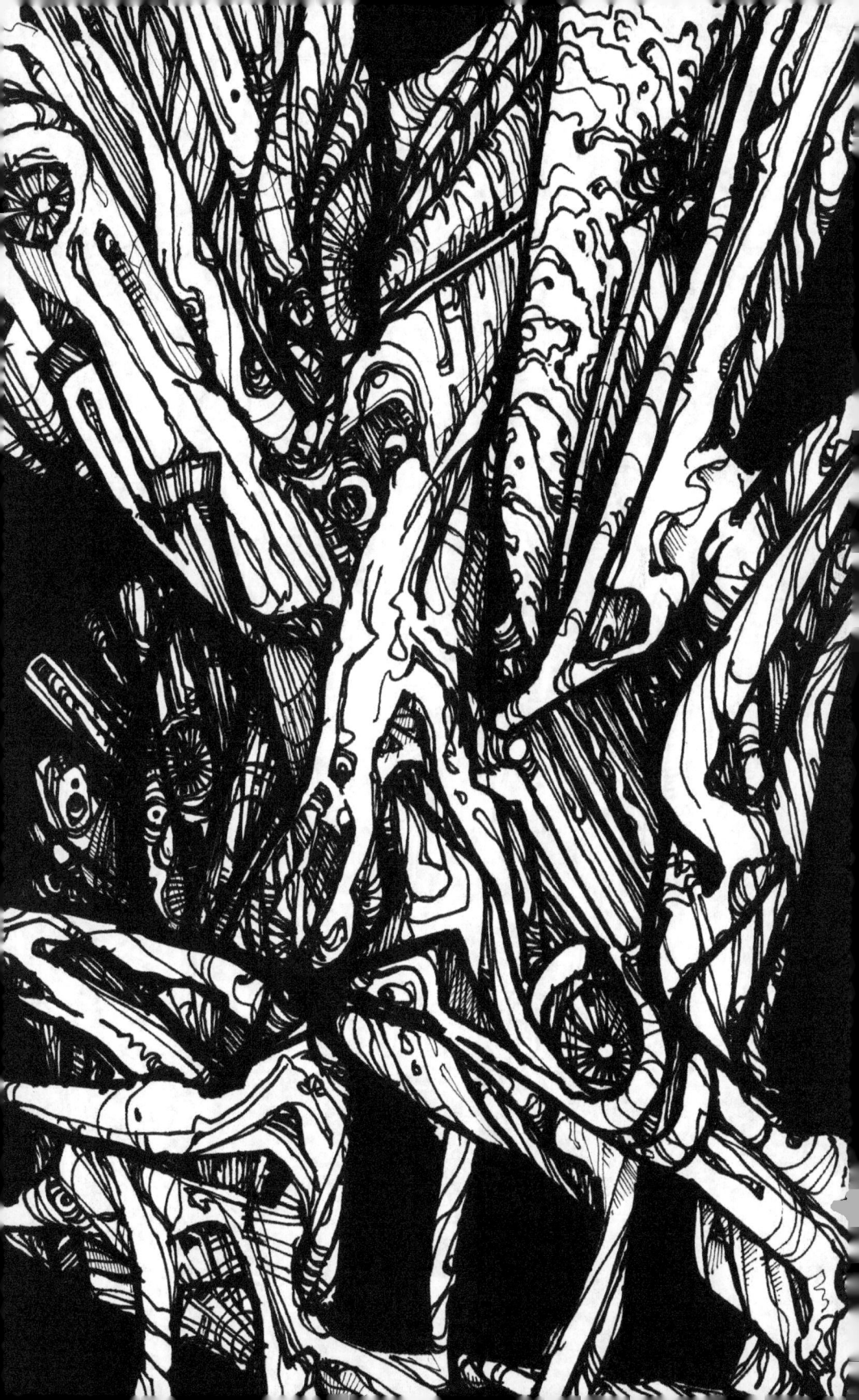

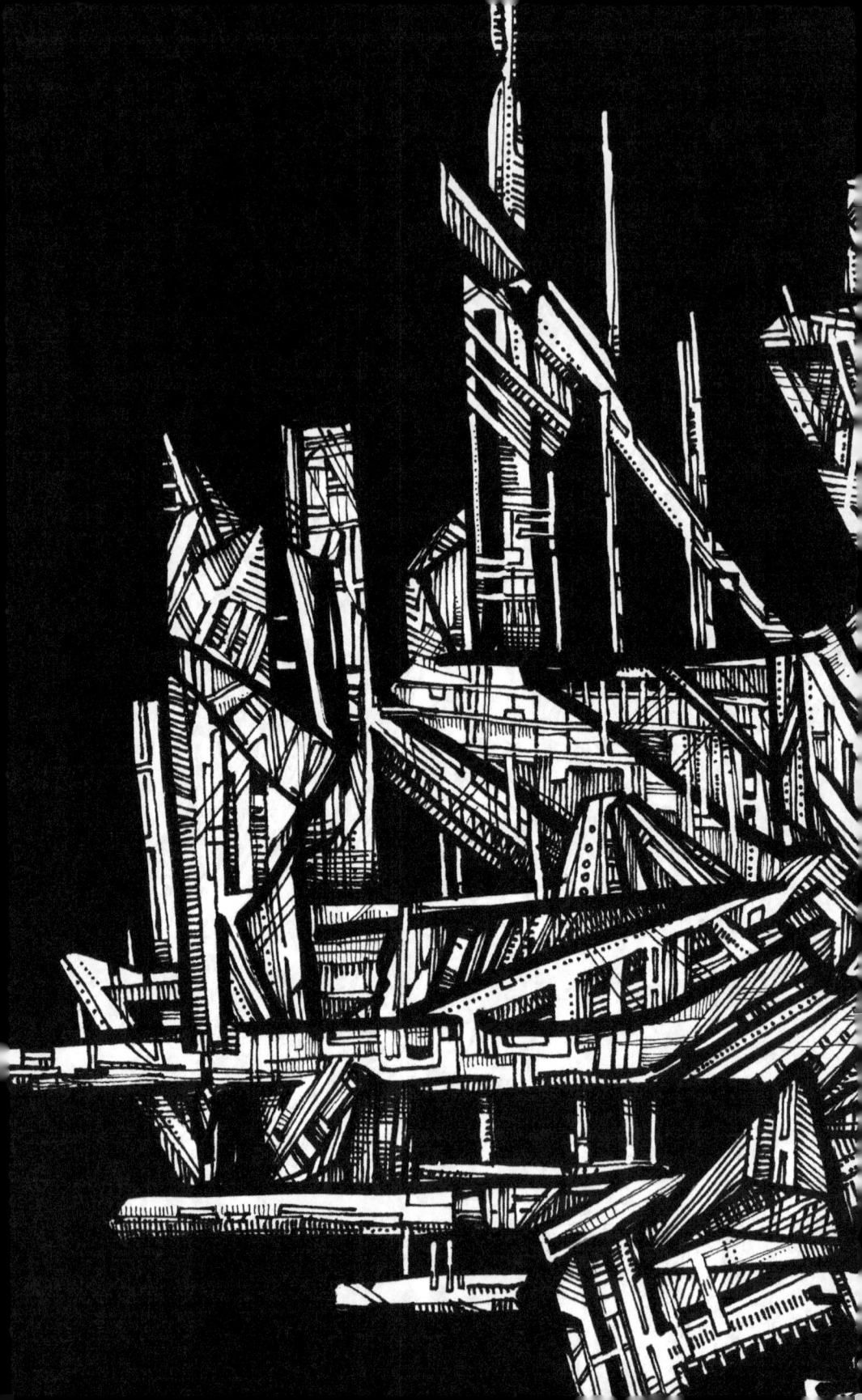

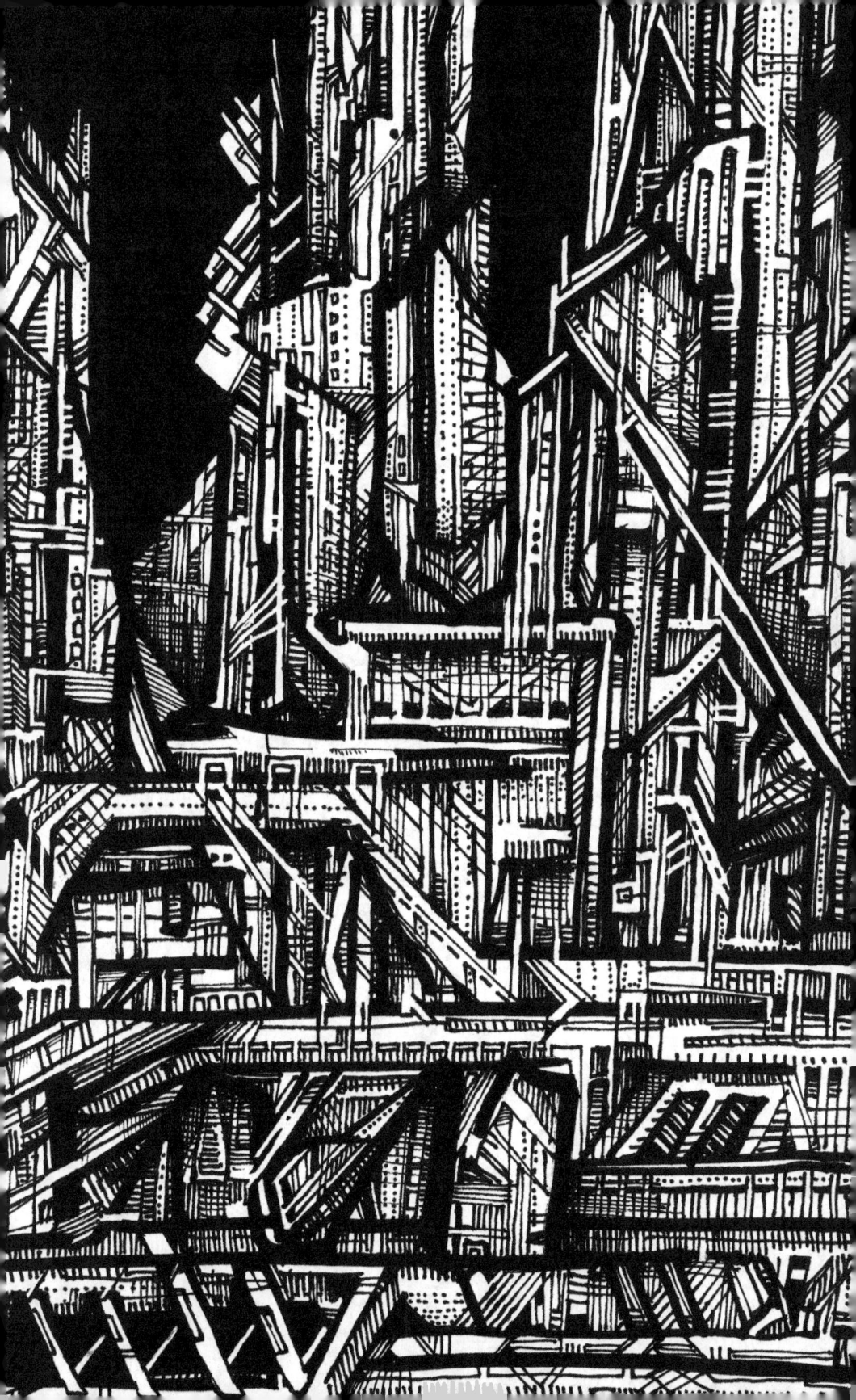

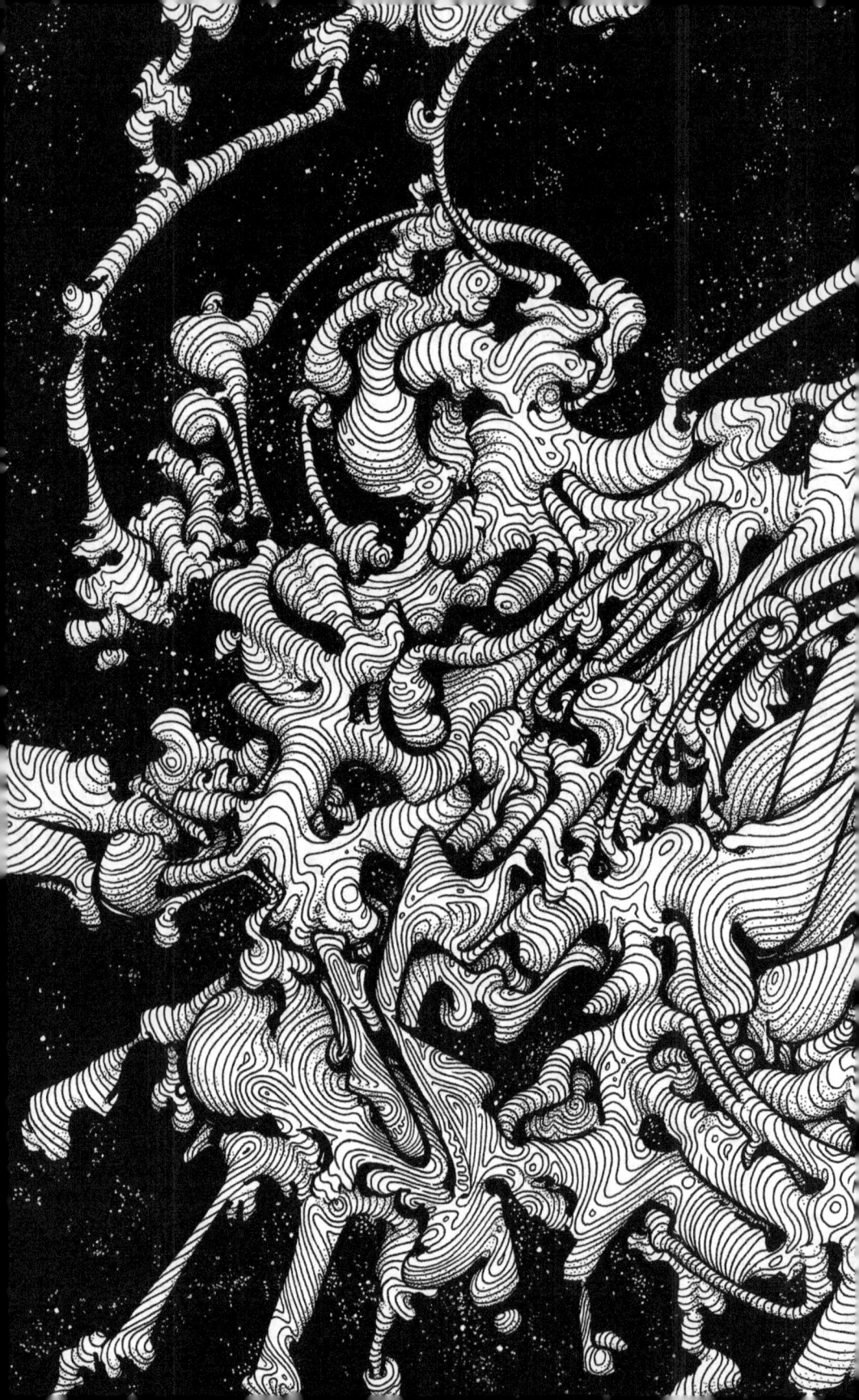

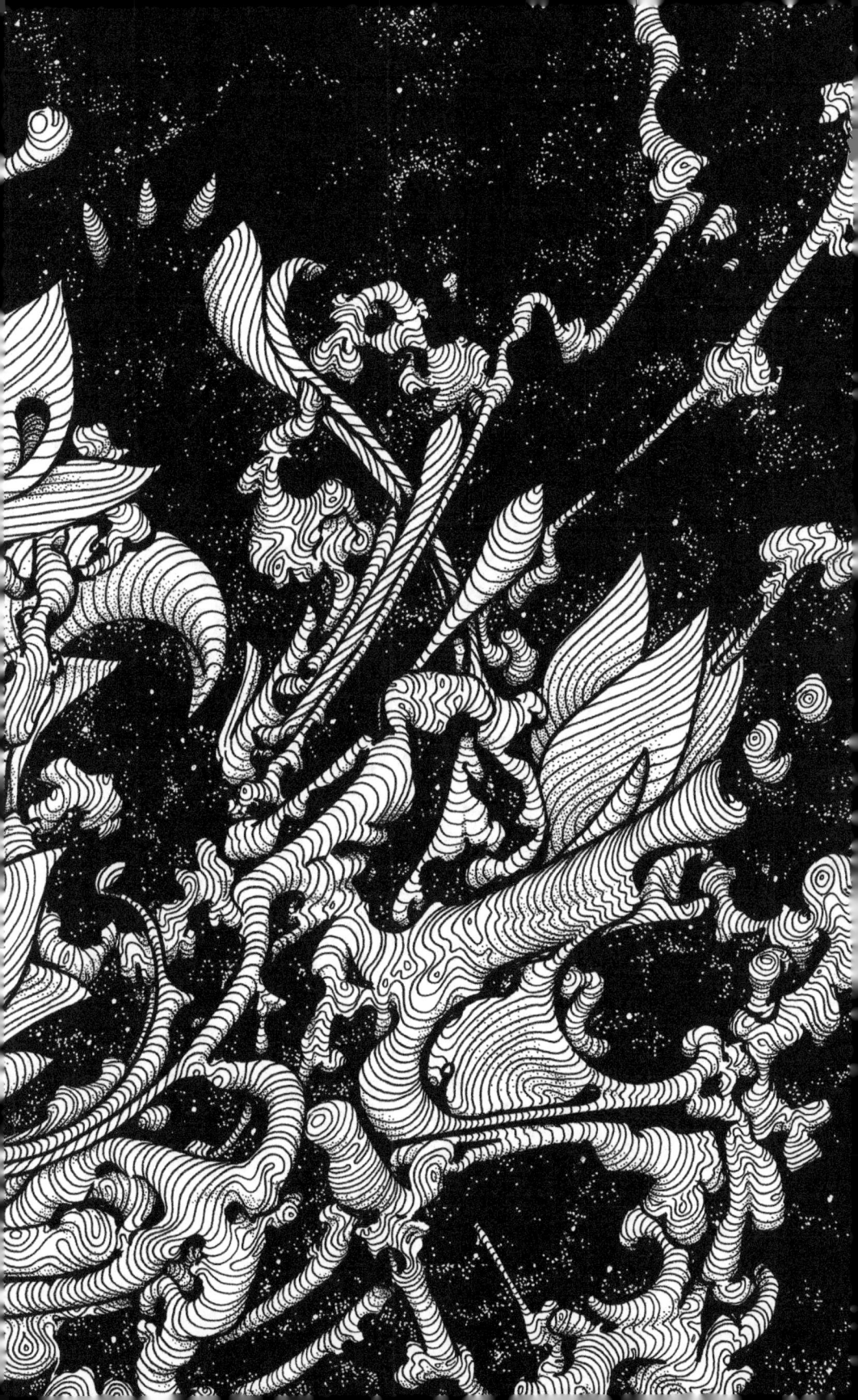

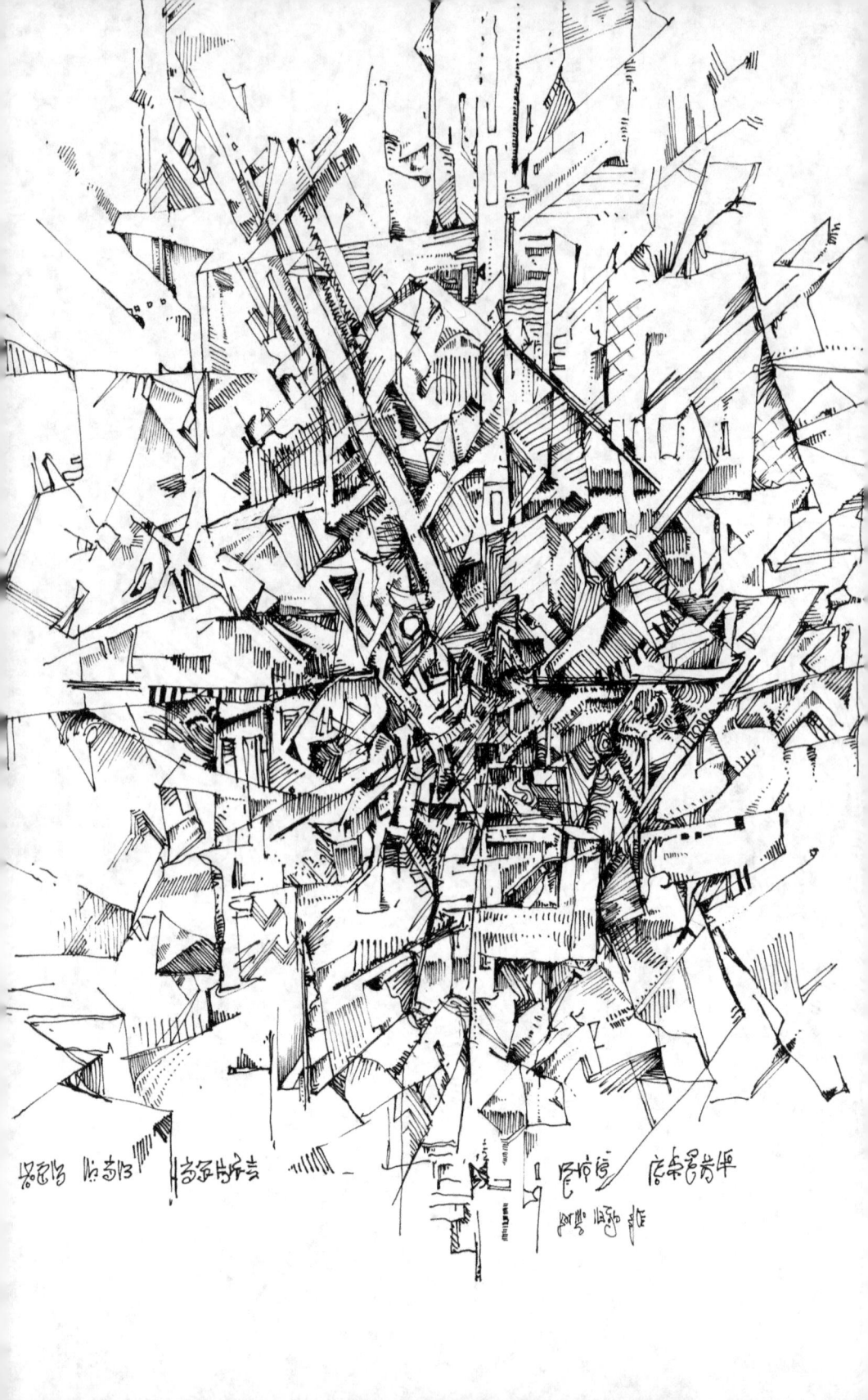

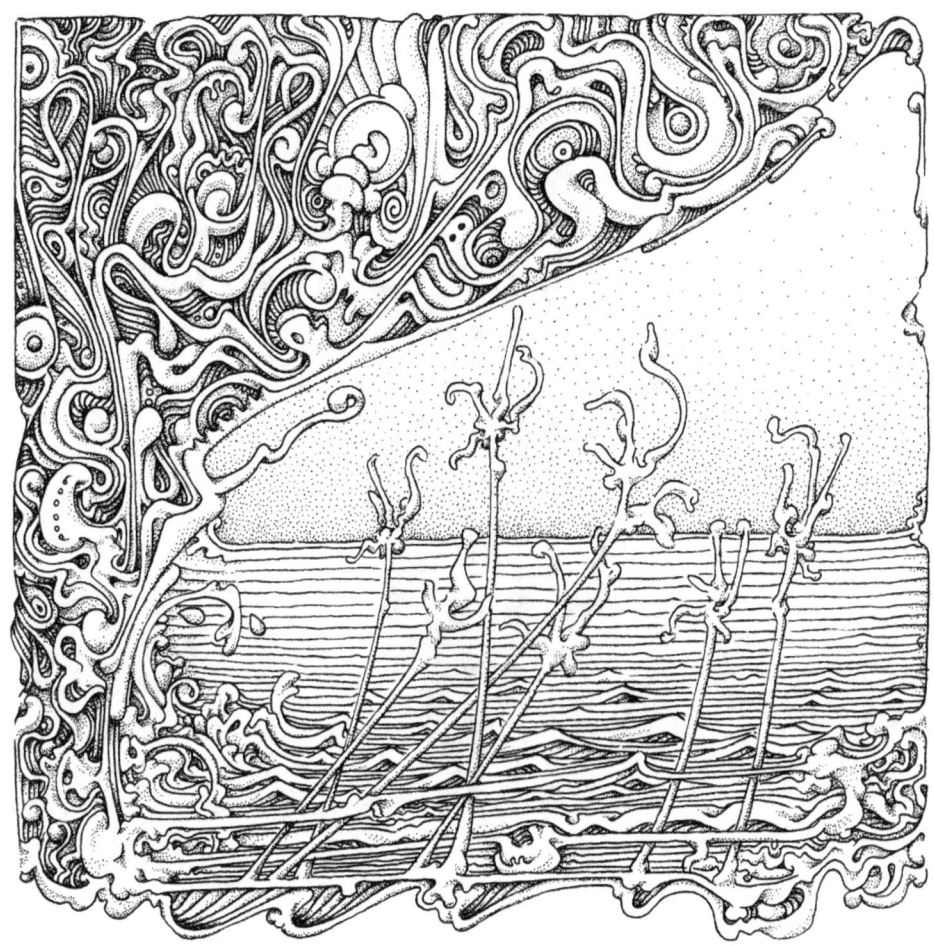

STEPPING IN FROM THE BACK PORCH I CLOSED
THE SCREEN DOOR BEHIND ME AND MENTIONED
THAT maybe SOMEONE SHOULD GO GET MORE
TRASH BAGS FROM THE STORE & ALTHOUGH it REALLY
WAS JUST A THOUGHT IN PASSING ITS AUDIBLE
PRESENCE MADE ME REALIZE
THAT THERE REALLY WERE ALMOST NONE LEFT
& THE LACK OF (DISAGReeMENT FROM ANY-
ONE ELSE PRESENT WAS TRULY AN...
ENCOURAGEMENT TO ME AND IMPROVED MY
MOOD SIGNIFICANTLY AS I WASHED THE
PLATE & THE BOWL & TRIMMED THE
SCRAGGLY FUZZIES FROM THE CARPET WITH
SOME FINGERNAIL CLIPPERS SO I COULD GET
DOWN ON THE SIDE of MY FACE AND LOOK
STRAIGHT ACROSS INTO THE EYES IN THE
BASE BOARD UNDER THE CHAIR THERE
WHERE I WONDERED IF THEY BLINKED
WHEN I BLINKED OR JUST WHEN I
LOOKED AWAY OR IF THEY COULD EVEN
SEE ANYTHNG LIKE I HOPED THEY
COULDN'T.

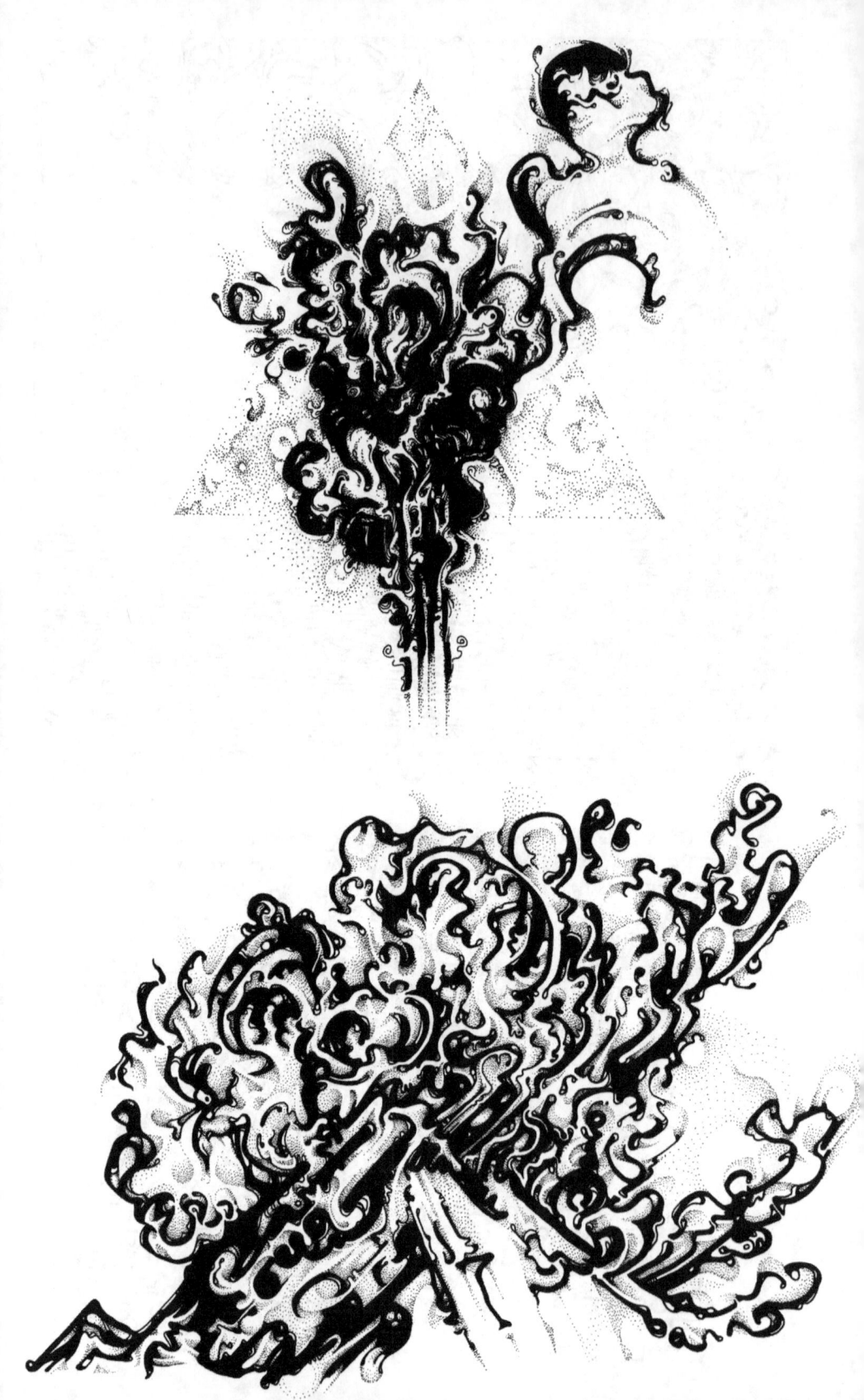

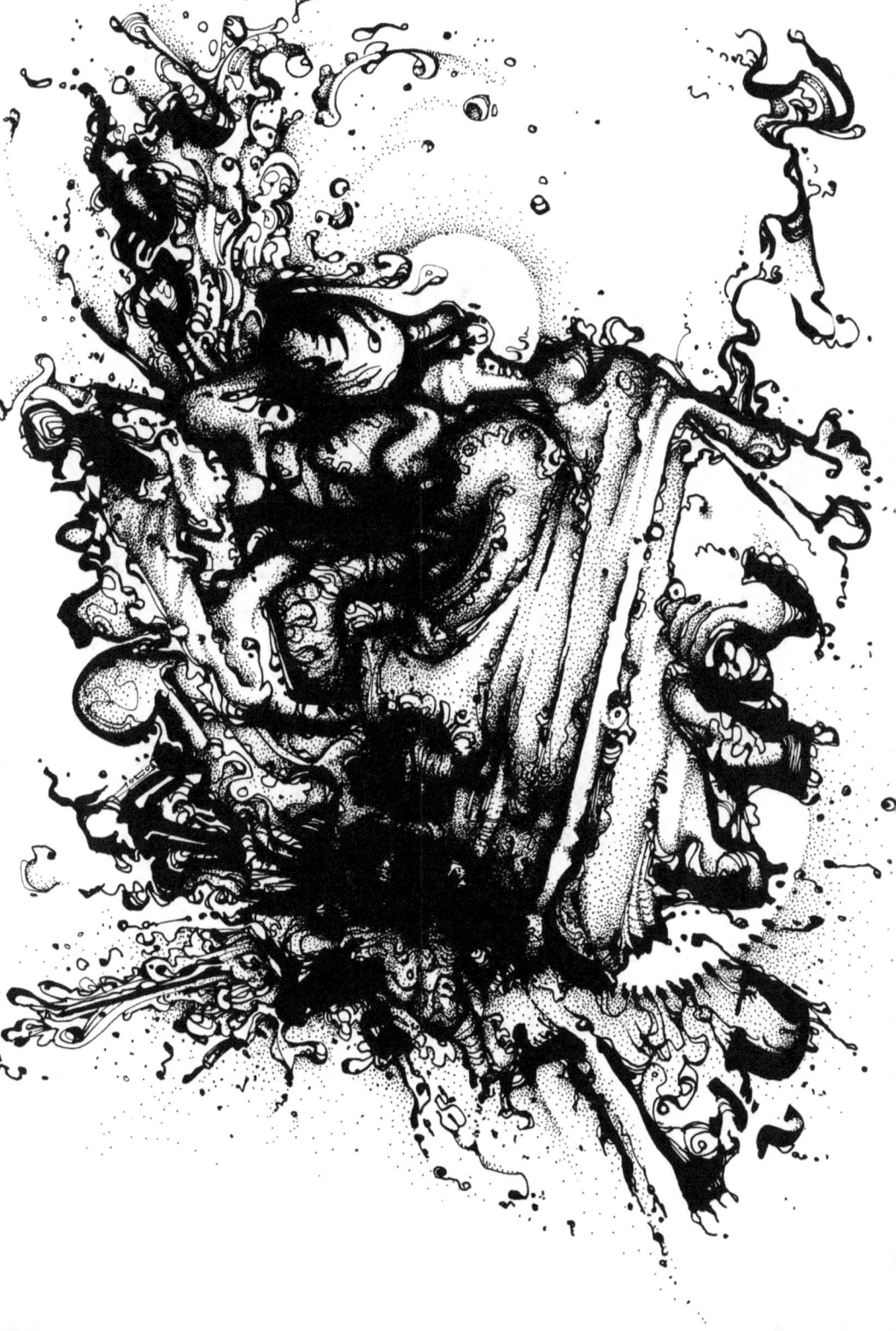

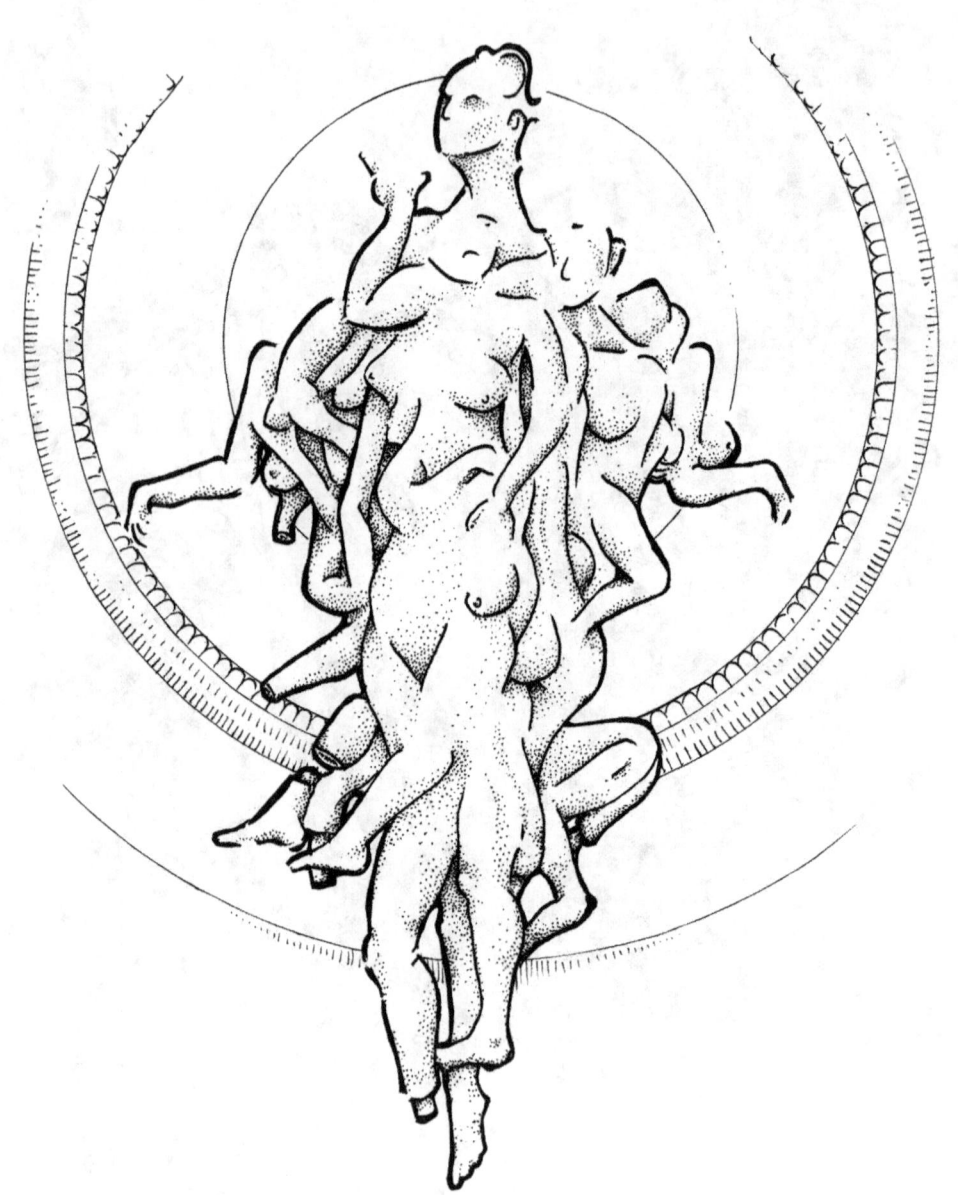

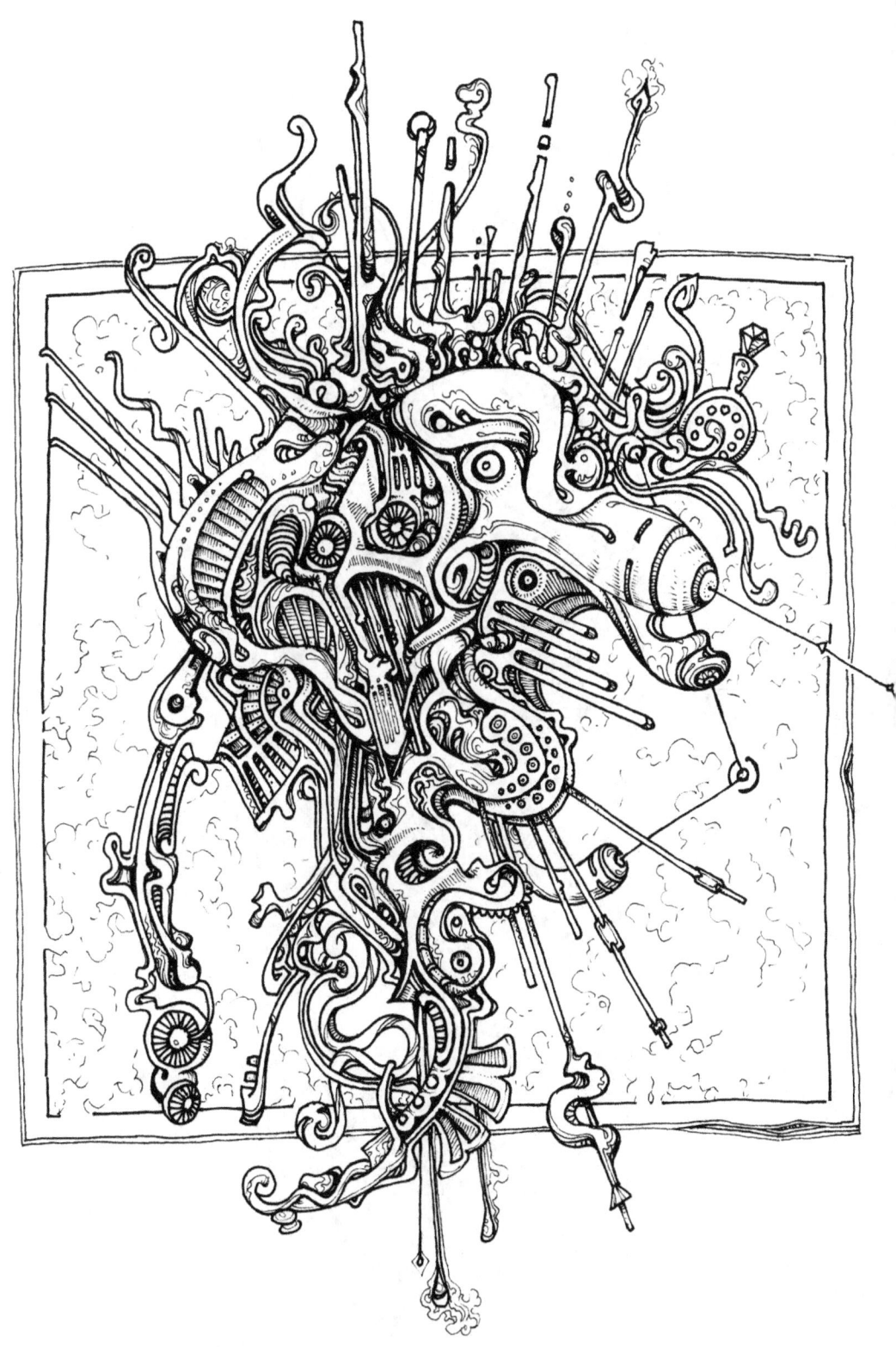

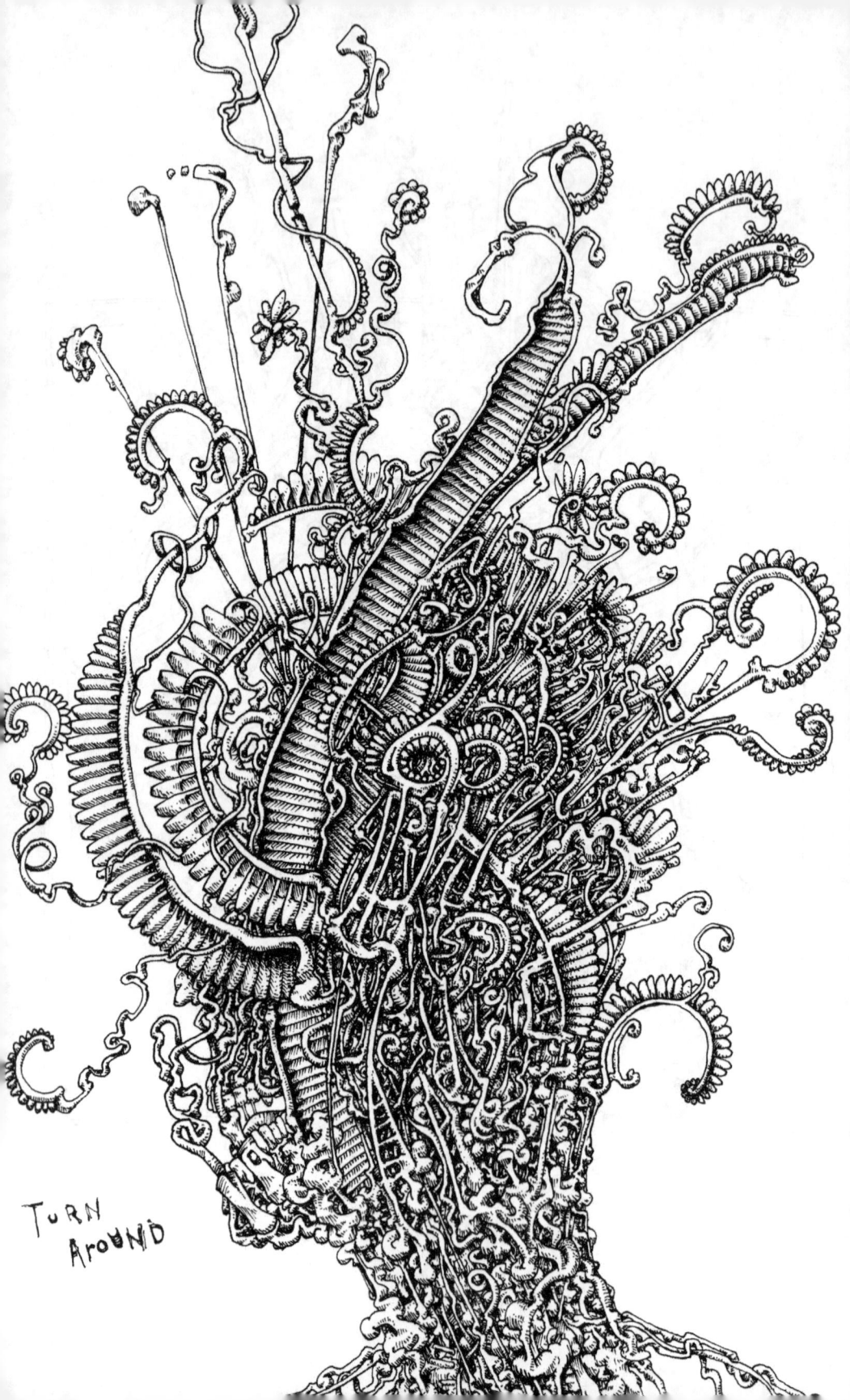

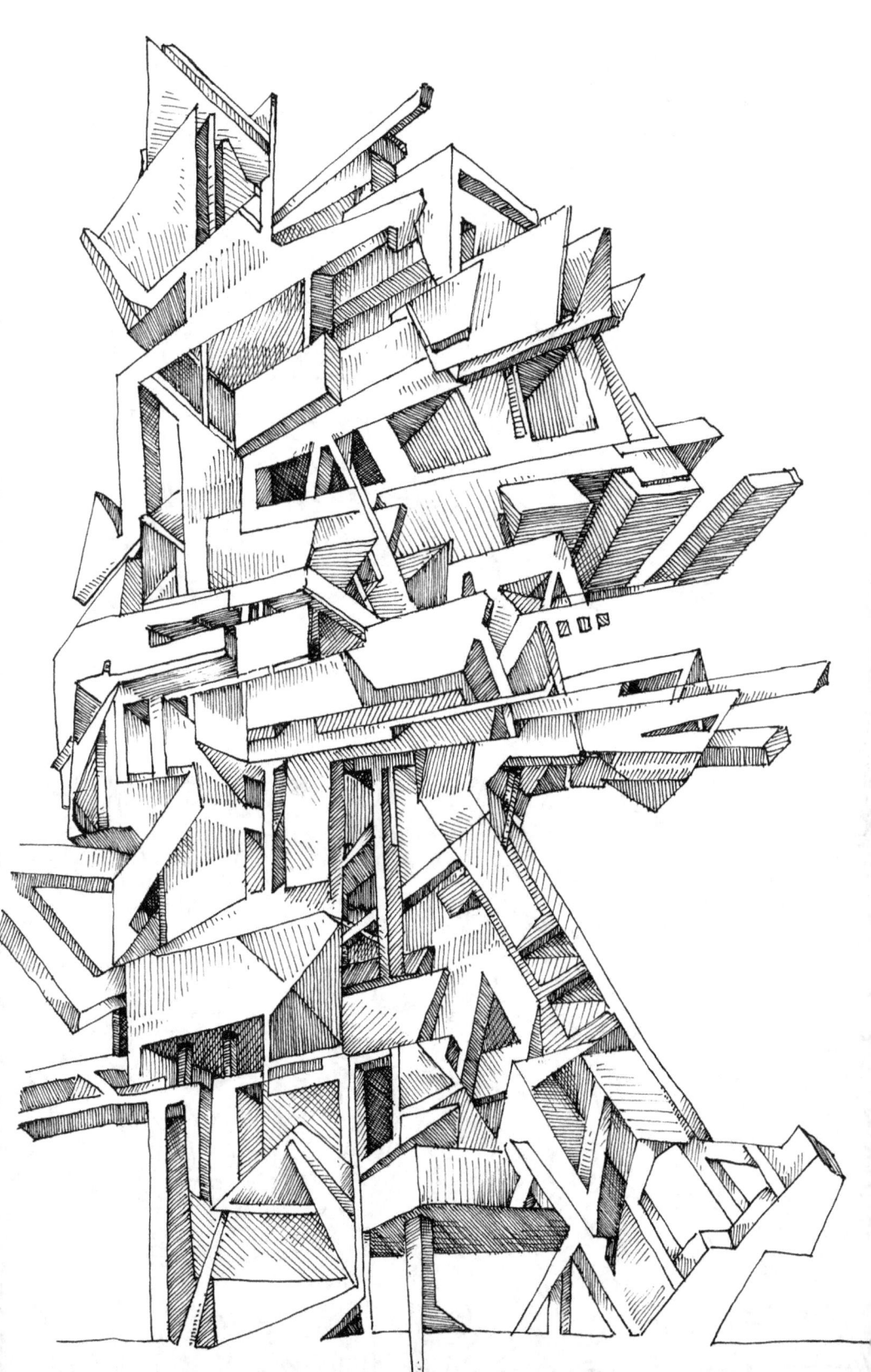

They felt strongly about the issues at hand so of course a strongly-worded letter didn't seem uncalled for or completely out of line and so just such a piece of correspondence was drafted up with great care to spare no murmuring word or smoulderous grudge from any of the choiry host gathererd there that hingeful day when the future swung open in the other direction and entire armies stepping in time tripped at once on the same uneven paving stone to that poor stone's untimely demise.

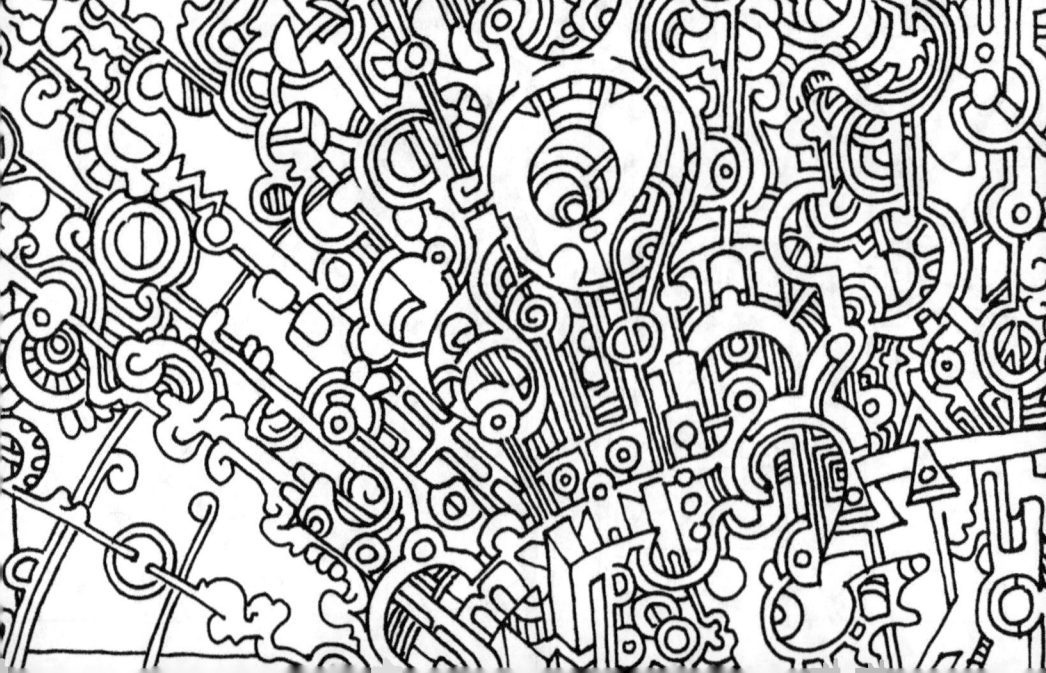

Scribbling furiously through the night and into
   the brick wall of the morning when all the
      fresh loaves of bANANA bREAD slowly slice
themselves obediently in some hidden rhythm
known ONLY to those churning tHE soon-to-be
butter at the mills in the hills where the river
   snakes through and People on paddleboats
                              scoff
      at pedestrians with cat-sized dogs and short
pants in floral prints reminiscent of gardens
   no one's ever tended or strolled through
pondering
      the purpose of all those pagodas and
         gazebos scattered across the face of
   the earth left empty except for an
also empty umbrella stand glistening in
the early dawn sun rays slanting
      through the recent holes
               in that wall.

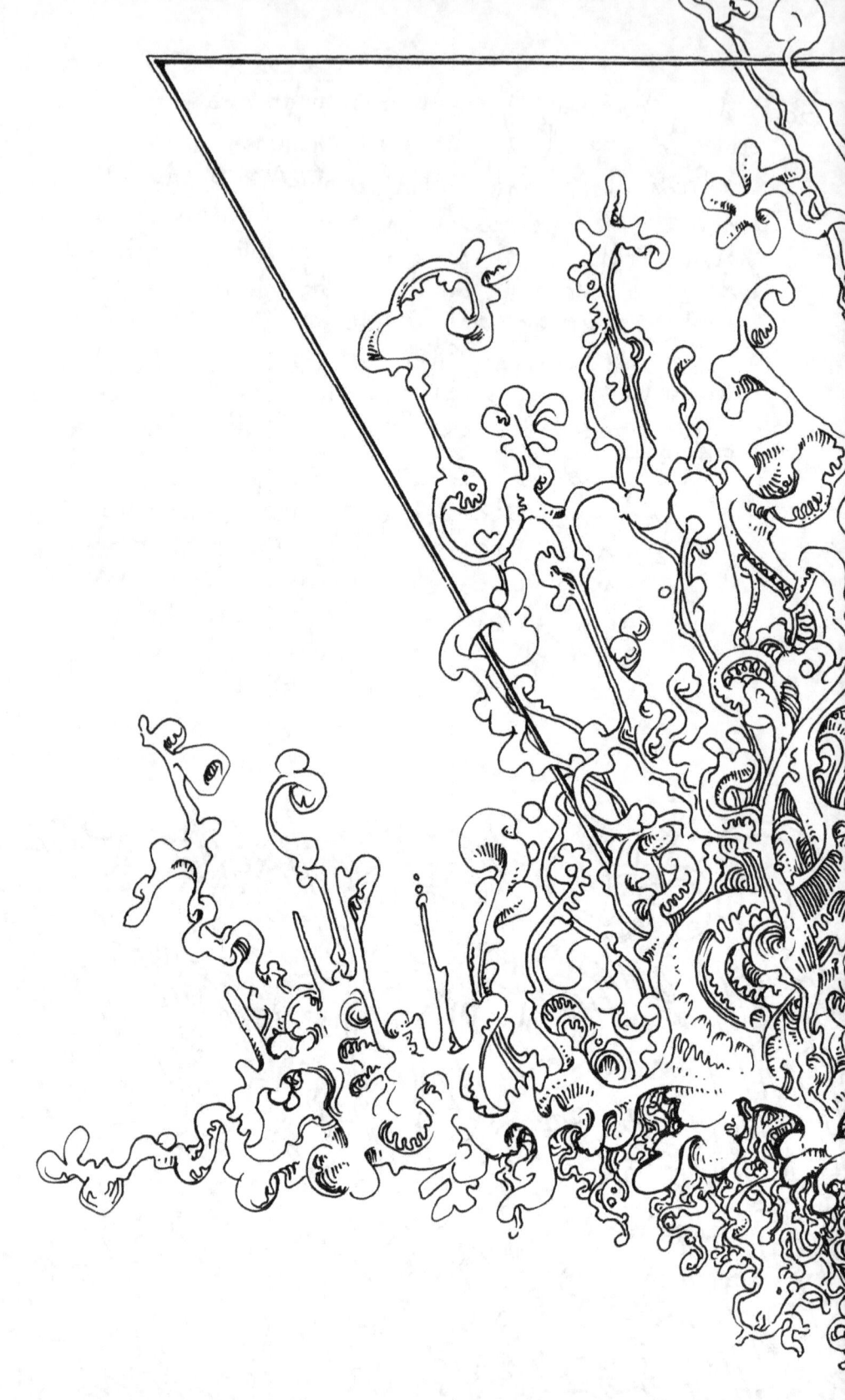

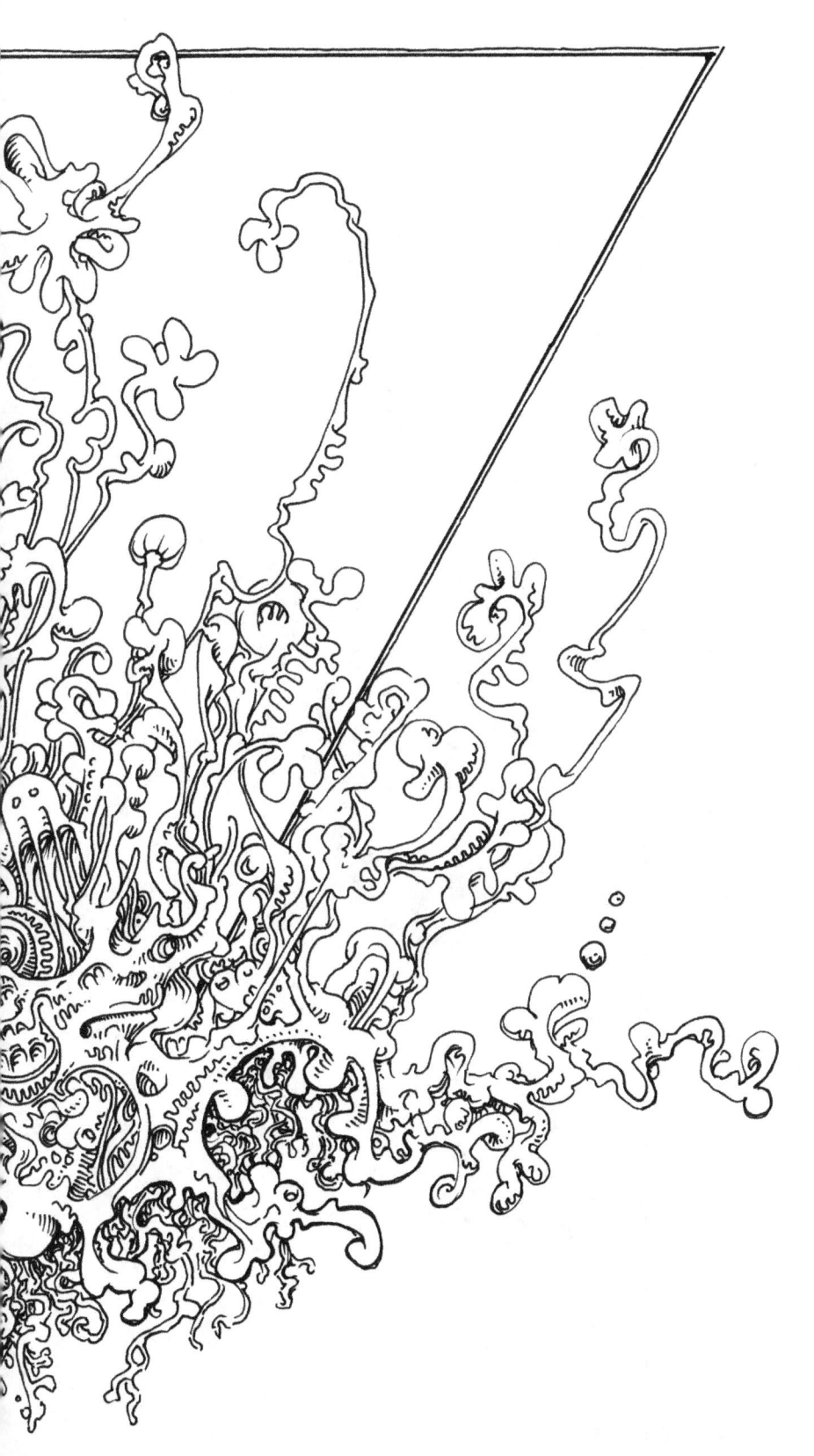

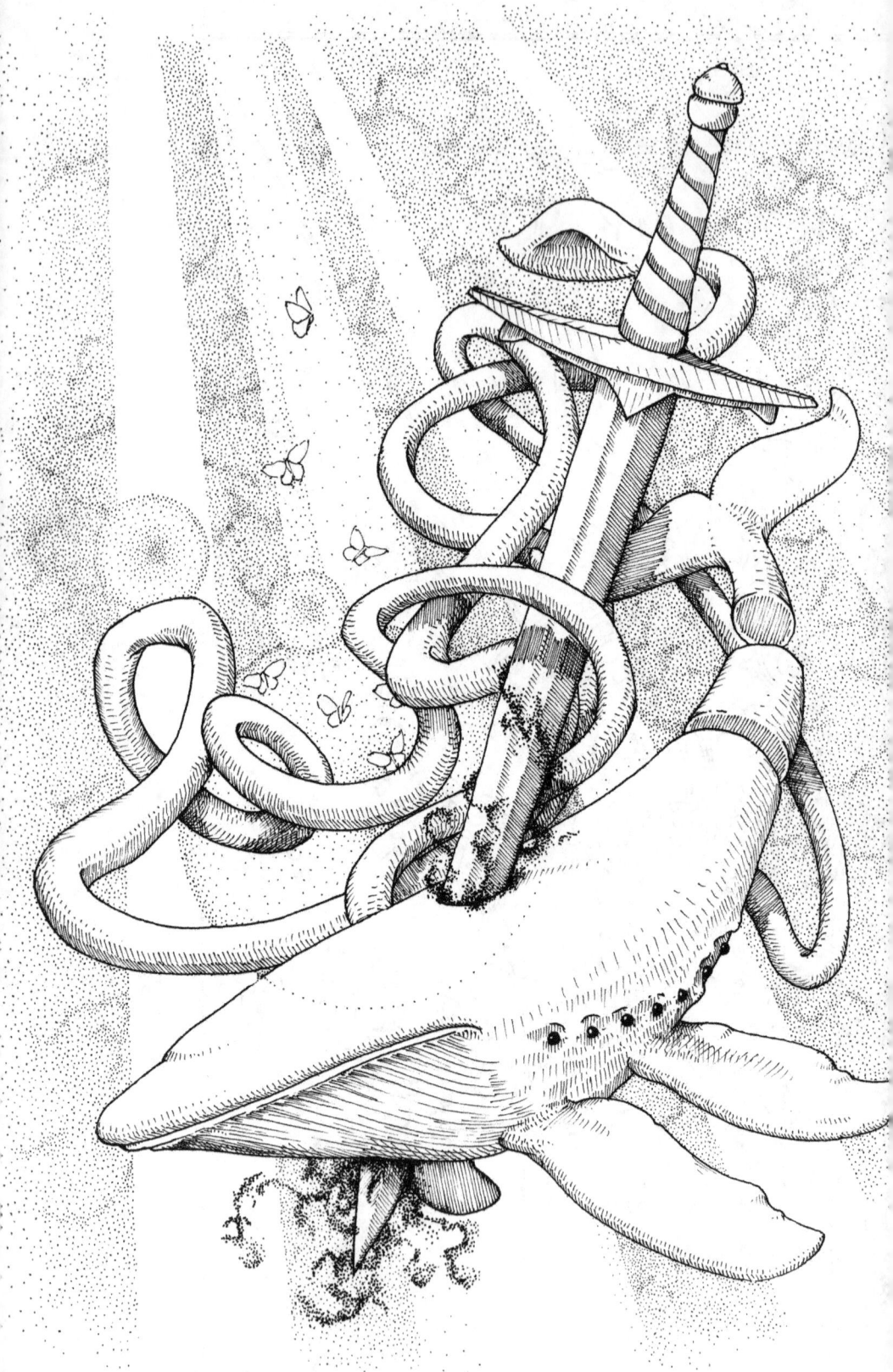

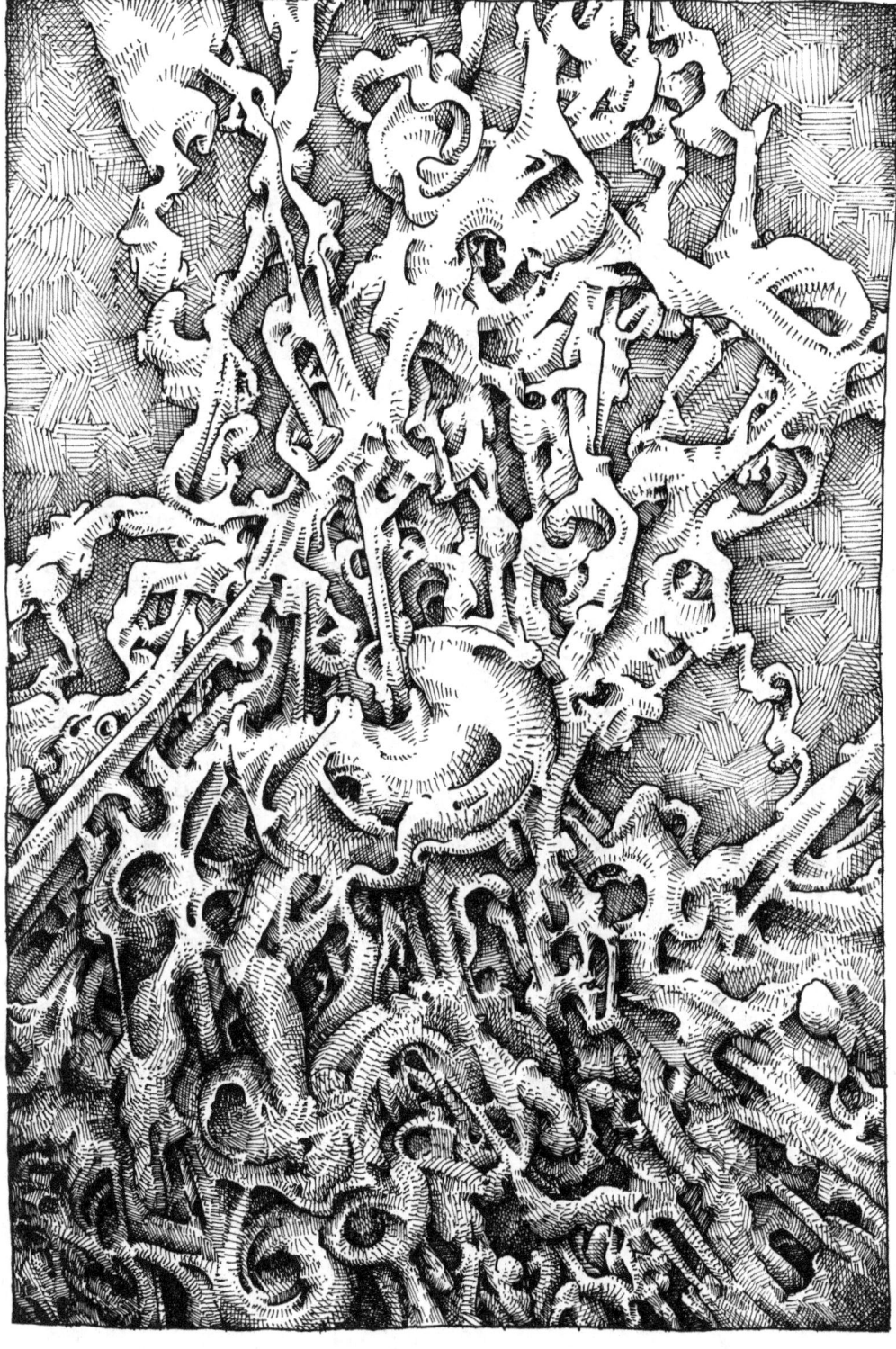

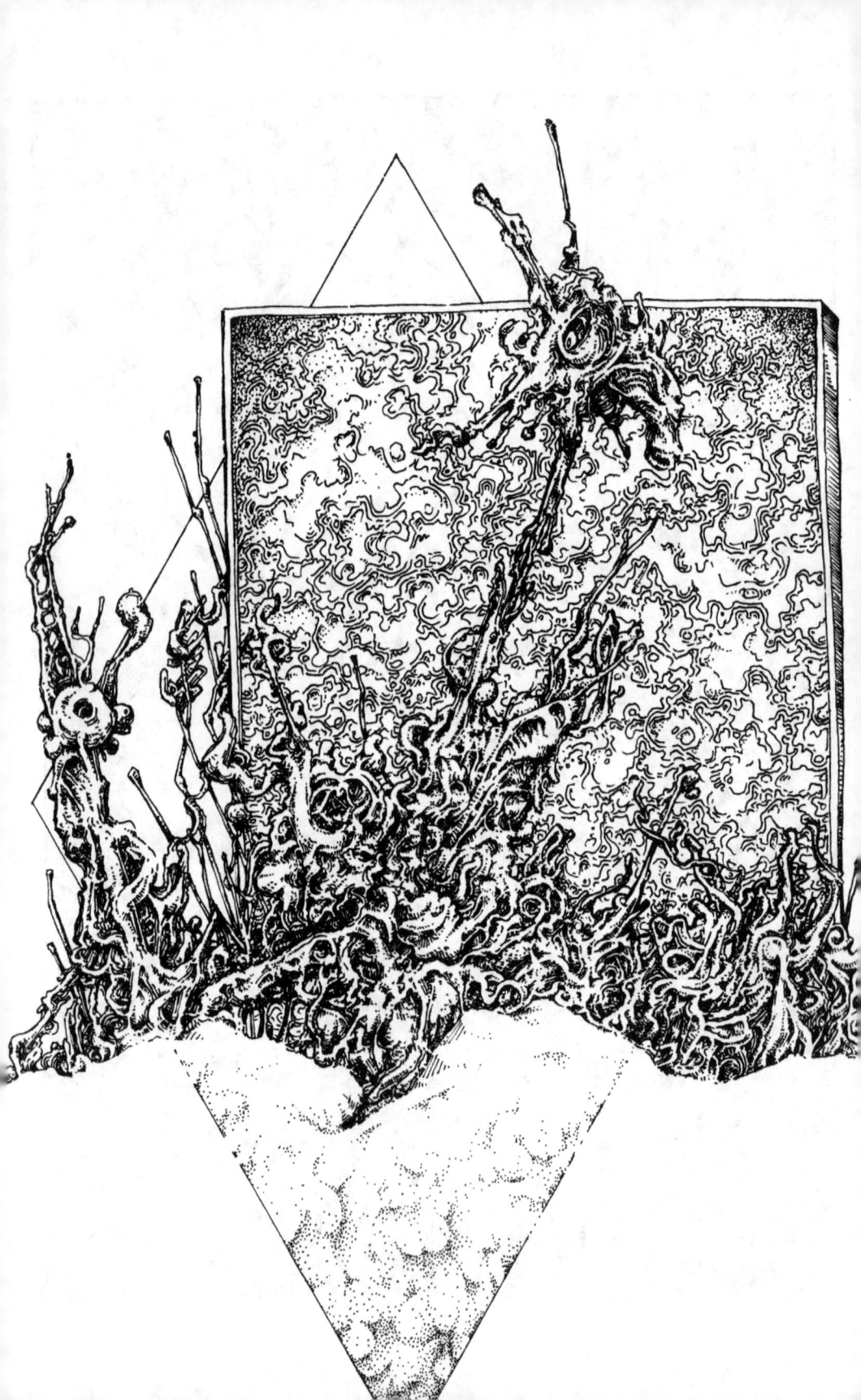

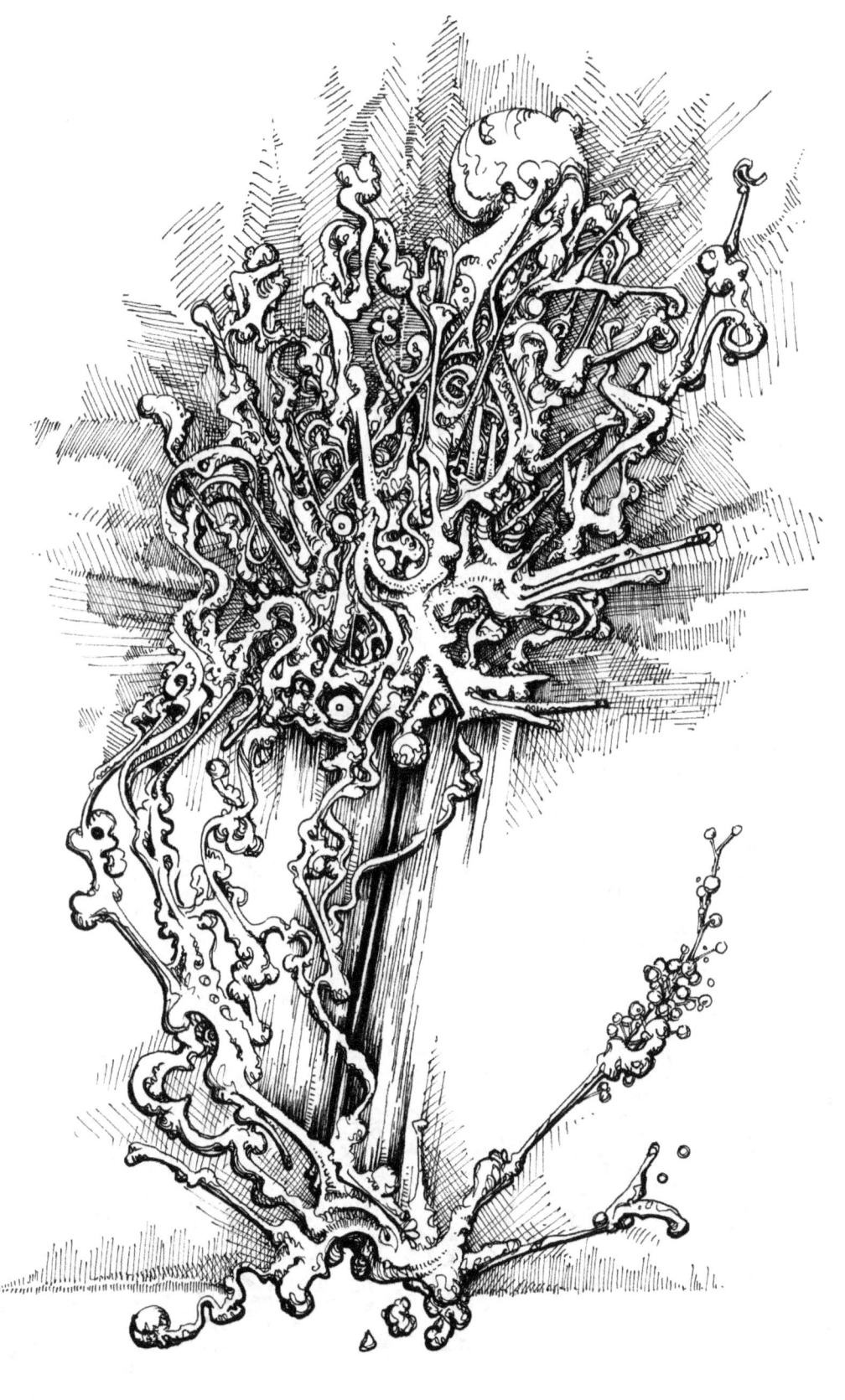

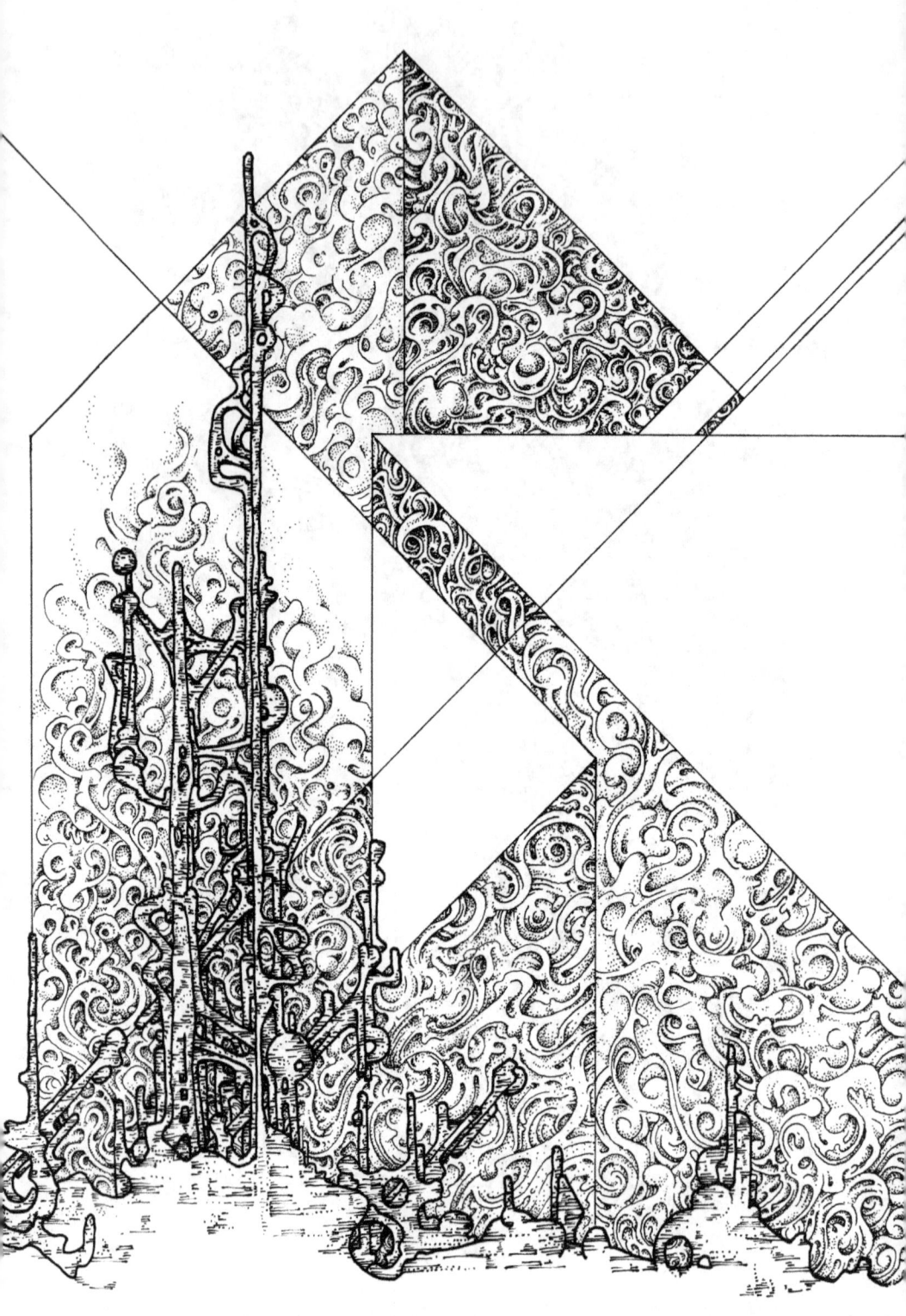

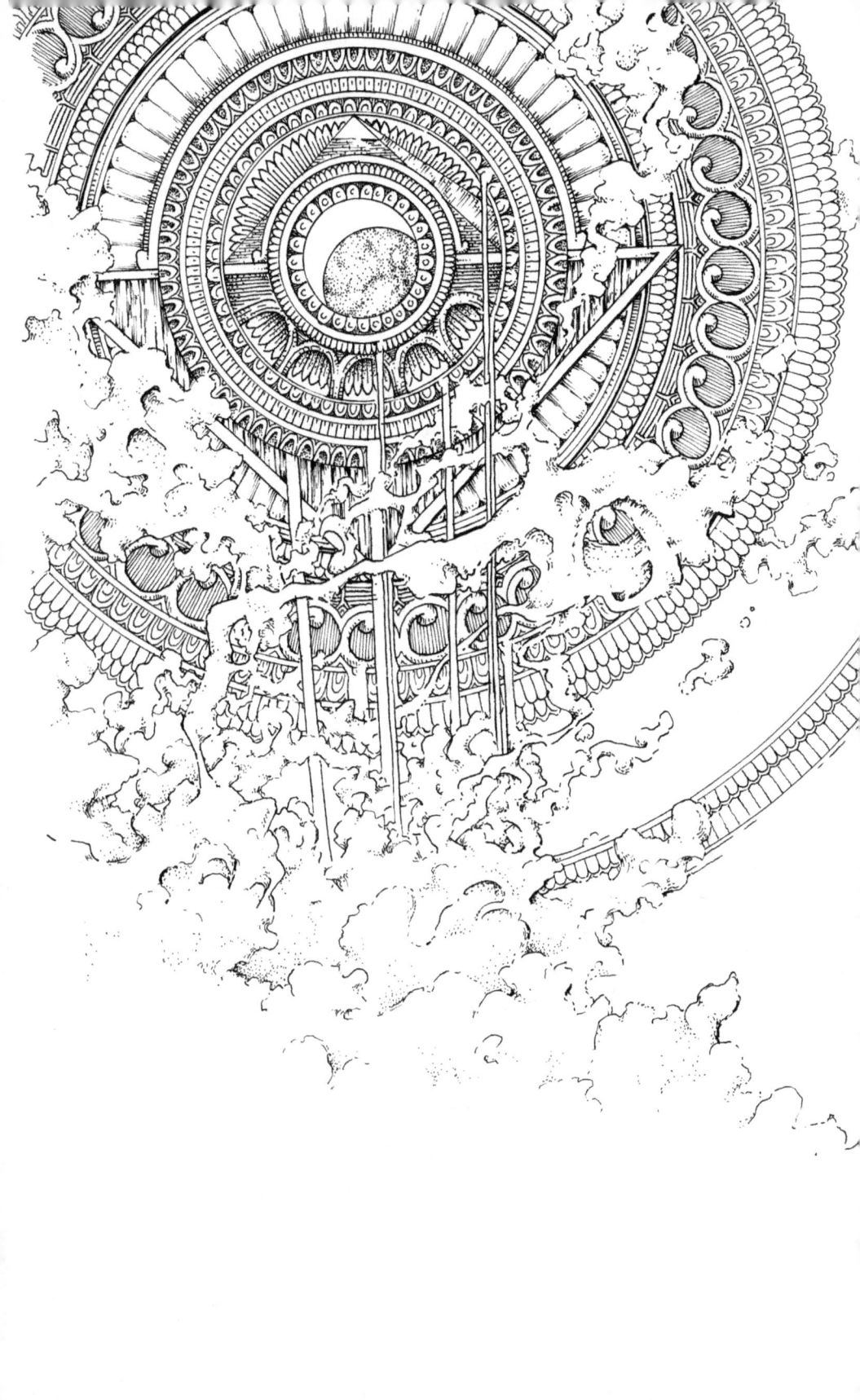

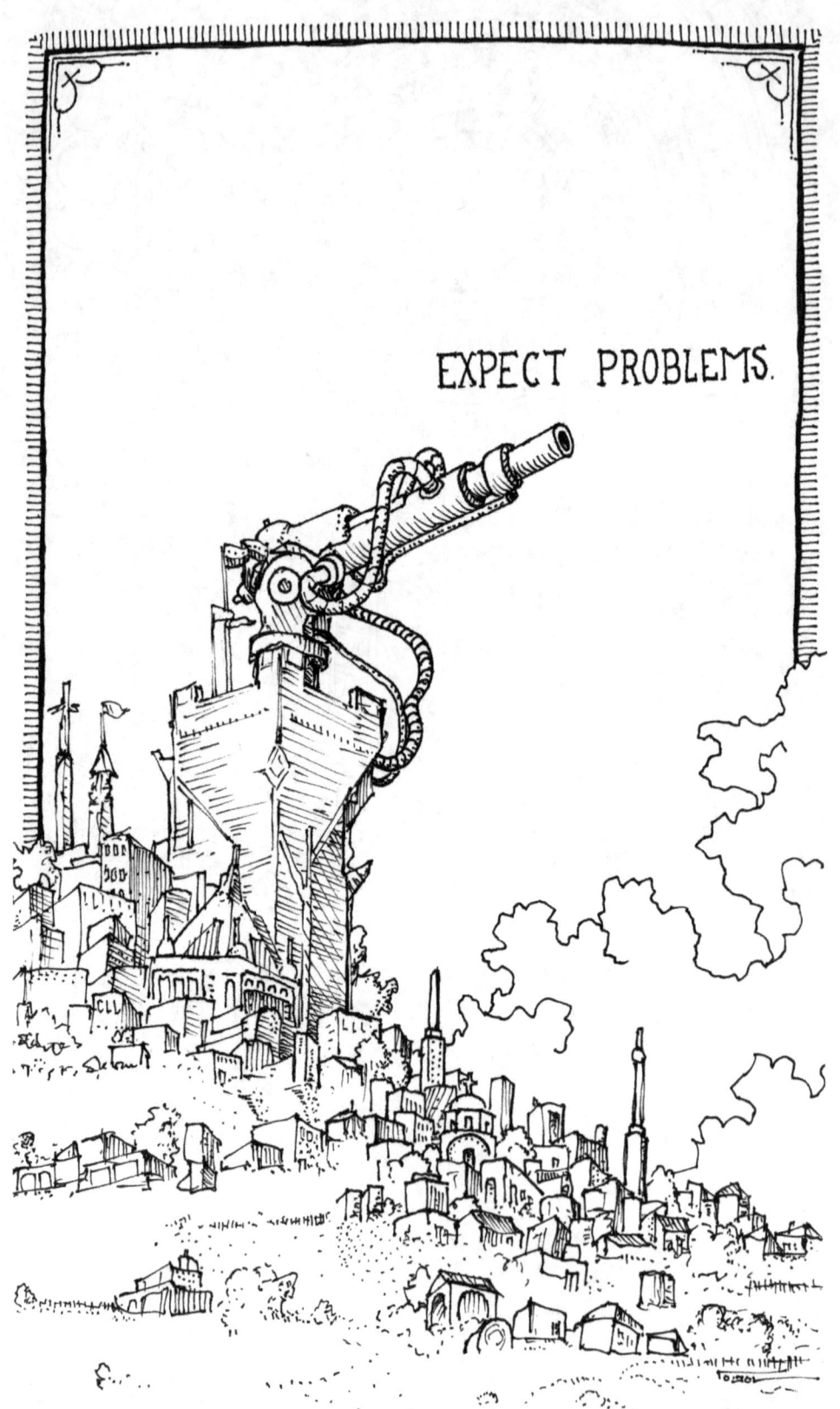

EXPECT PROBLEMS.

I was a little uncomfortable at the prospect of doing so many of these experiments by myself with so little formal experience so I bought some ad space on a local bathroom stall in a hasty scrawl that would hint at the urgency of having the position filled and sure enough before the year was out I had gone through no less than twelve hundred lab assistants in the process of taking that idyllic spring windowsill sunlight that's so inviting to hot pies and lonesome sighs and turning it into something a little more tangible and marketable by running the golden stuff through a series of prisms and hosiery and extruded foils in a technique I developed through trial and error and although I was proud of it I'll admit that I and my assistants may not have been wearing all the appropriate safety gear at all times as I certainly noticed a severe and ever decreasing quality in my dreams both awake and asleep.

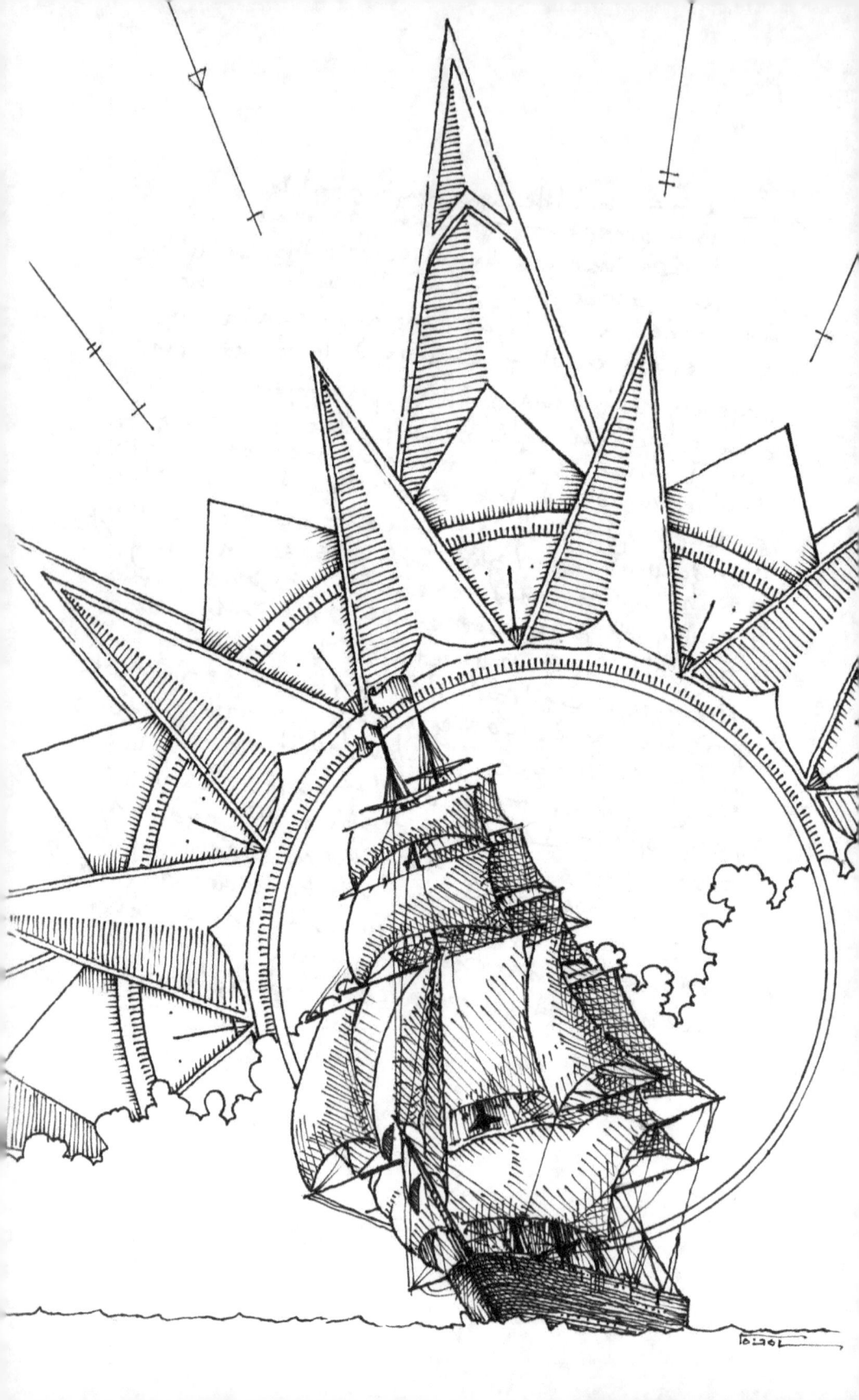

A few years ago a number of friends and I spent the summer wrapped up in a foolproof plan to make a quick buck by means of exploiting the utter dead-dog-on-a-hot-day exhaustion of the average workingman at the time and their instant willingness to throw a couple bucks at any problem to make it go away if it just meant they could mindlessly in- and exhale a couple more times before crawling back into those slatherous screaming chops again the second that relentless scorching star swung back around to shine what turned out to be a little more light than most people seemed entirely comfortable with despite their collective best efforts to raise a thick veil of choking billowy denial and heaving squinty progress in some direction that seemed vaguely profitable which was something I found myself really getting behind at the time in some misguided desire to break off a chunk of it for myself and hide it under the mattress where the beetles and worms would break it down and turn it into something useful or at least slightly less incriminating.

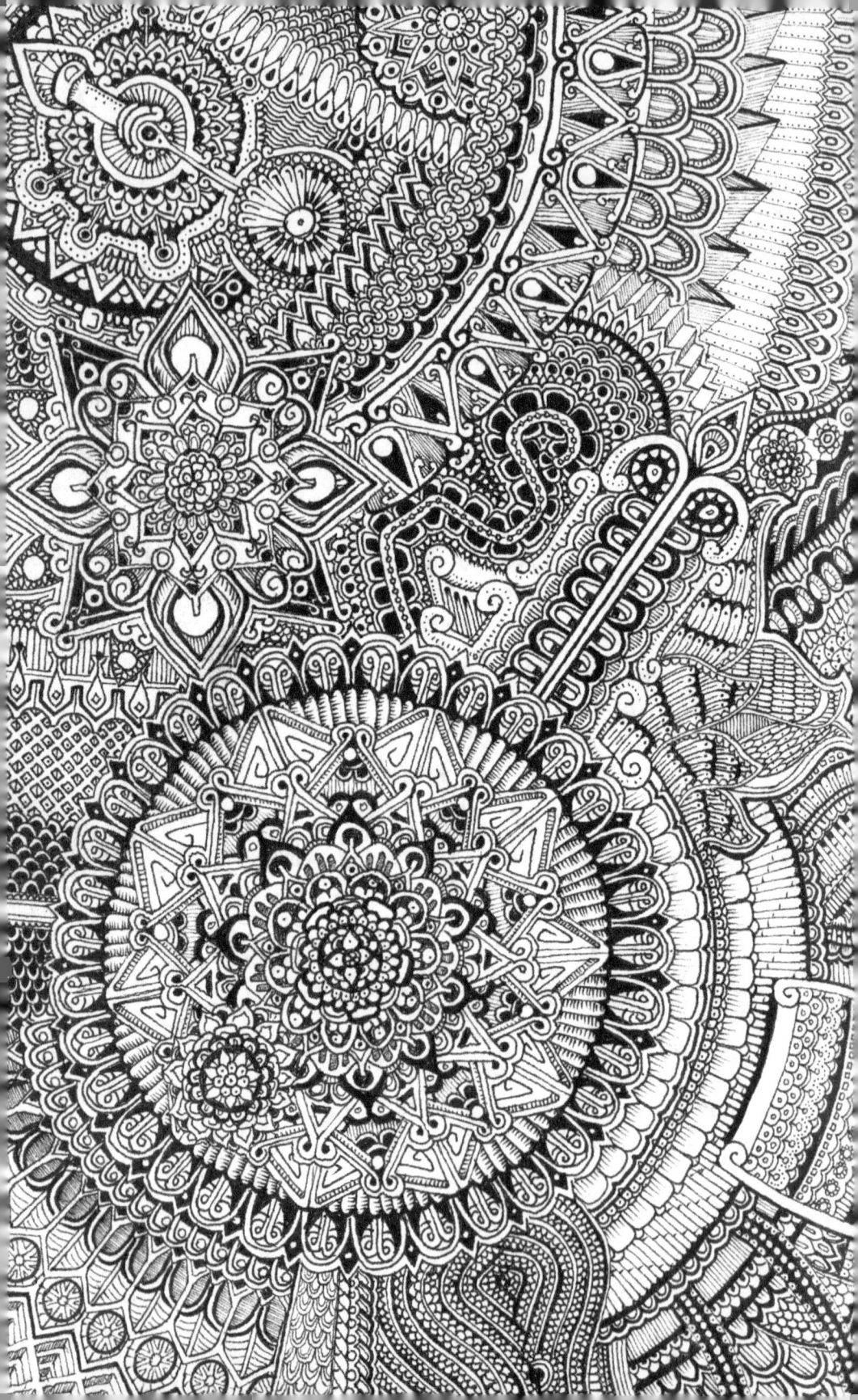

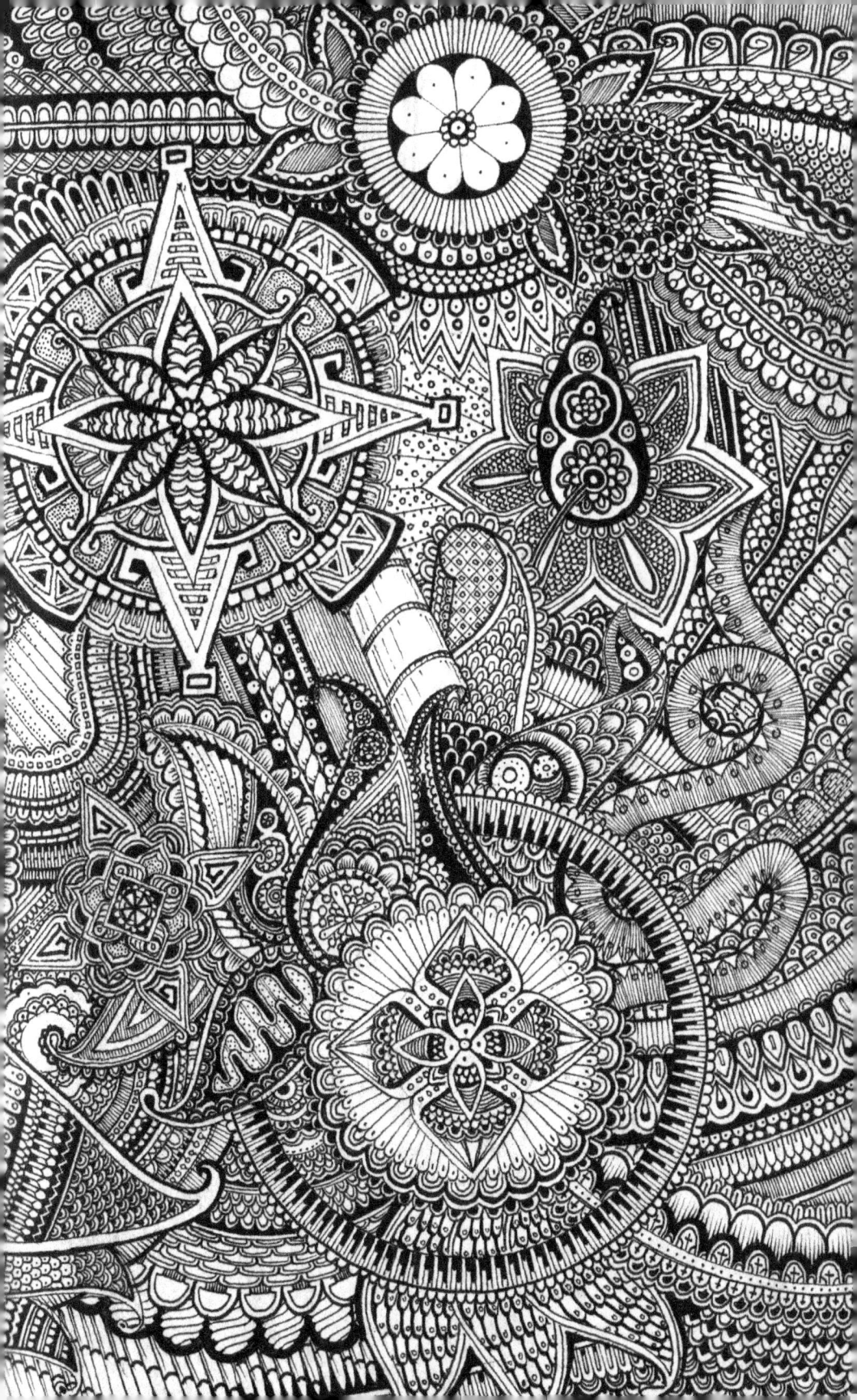

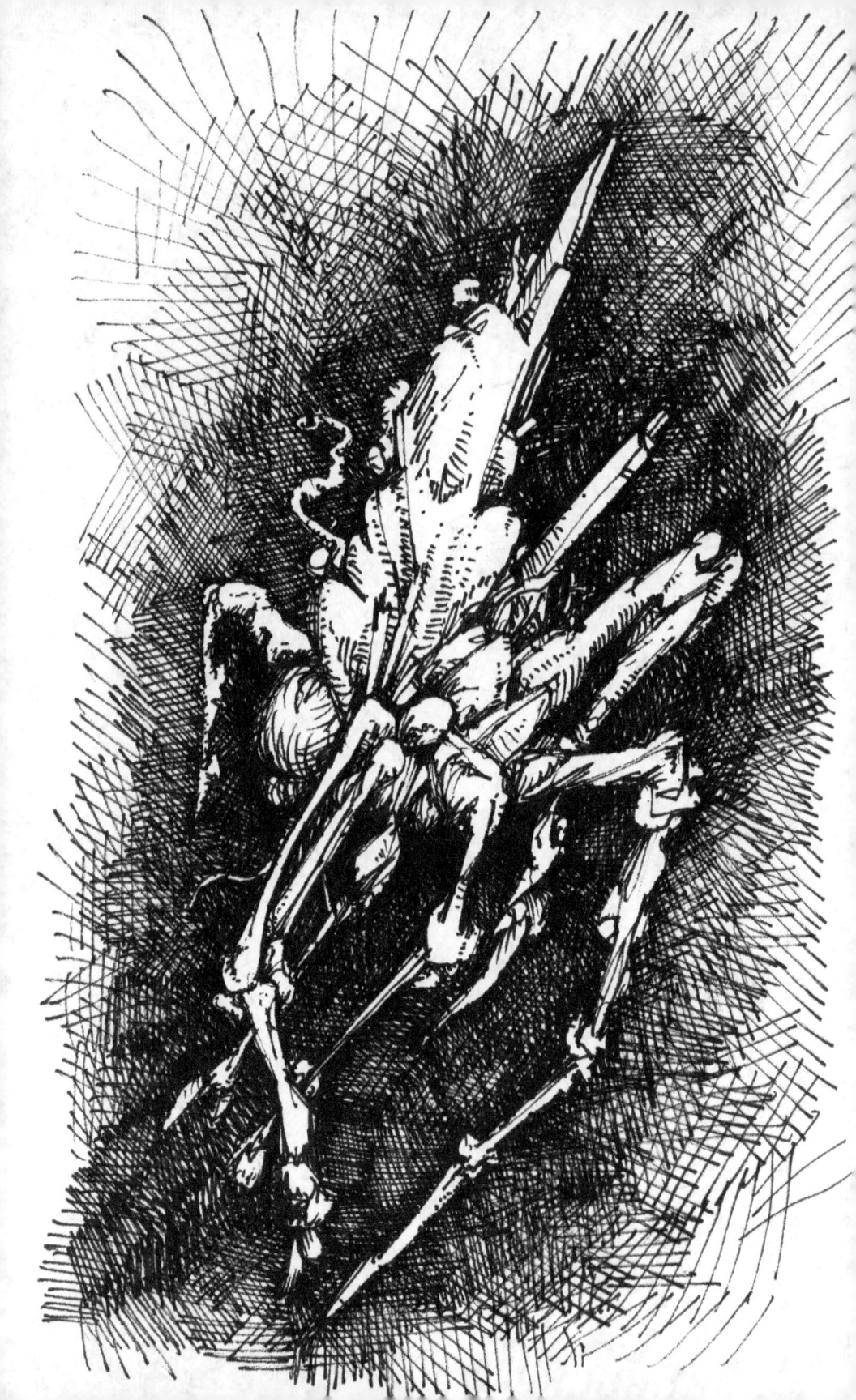

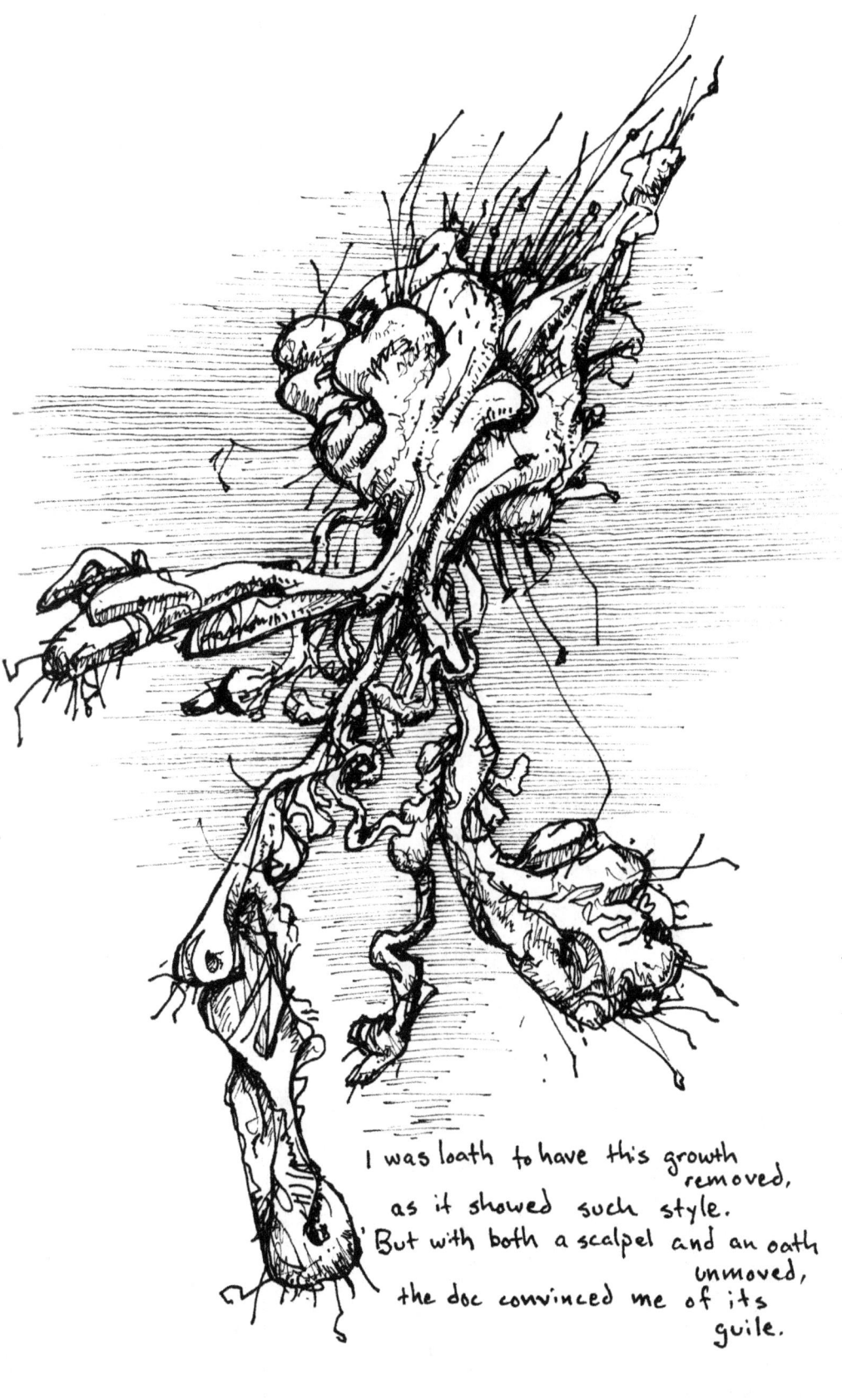

I was loath to have this growth
                removed,
    as it showed such style.
But with both a scalpel and an oath
                unmoved,
    the doc convinced me of its
                guile.

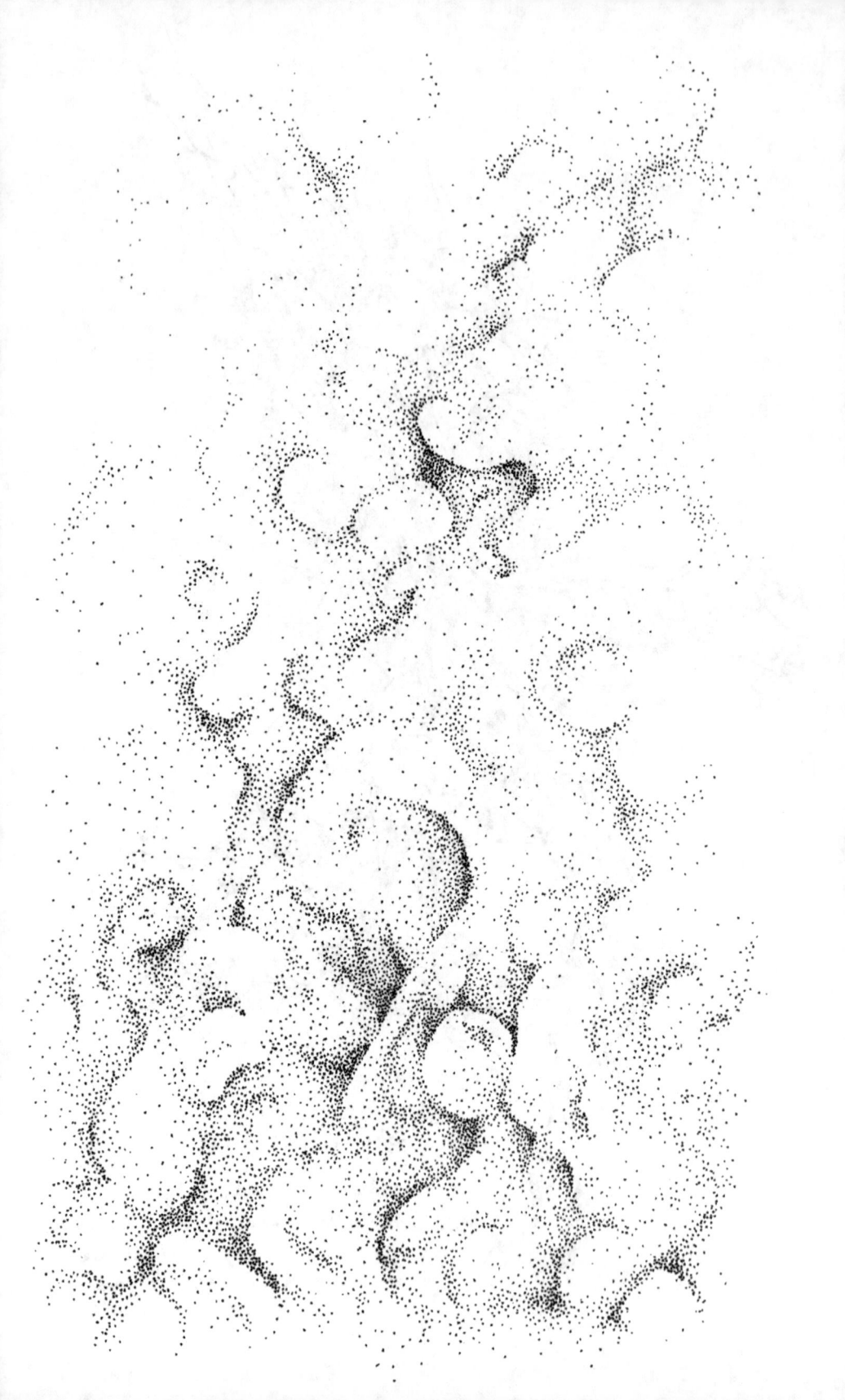

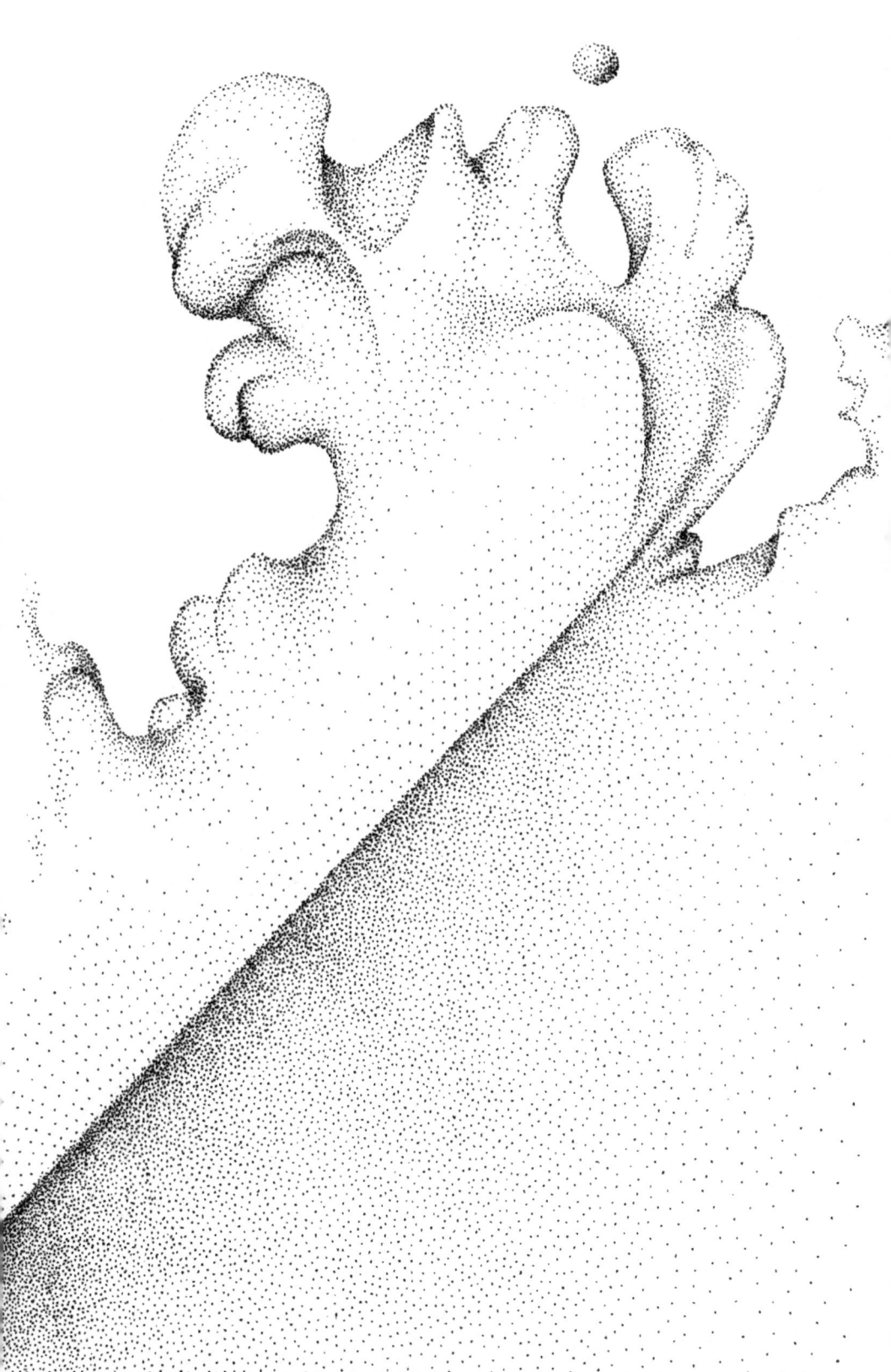

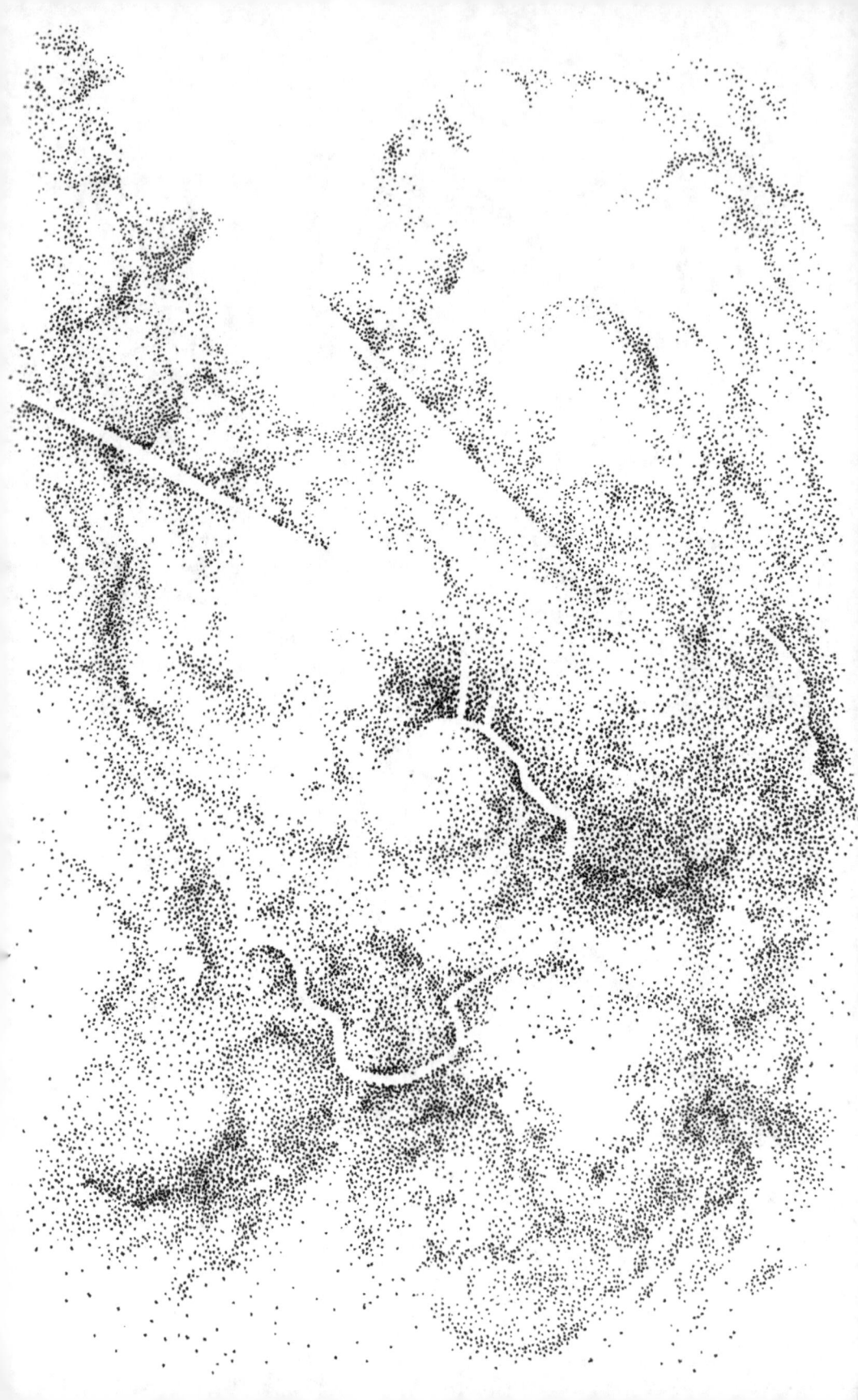

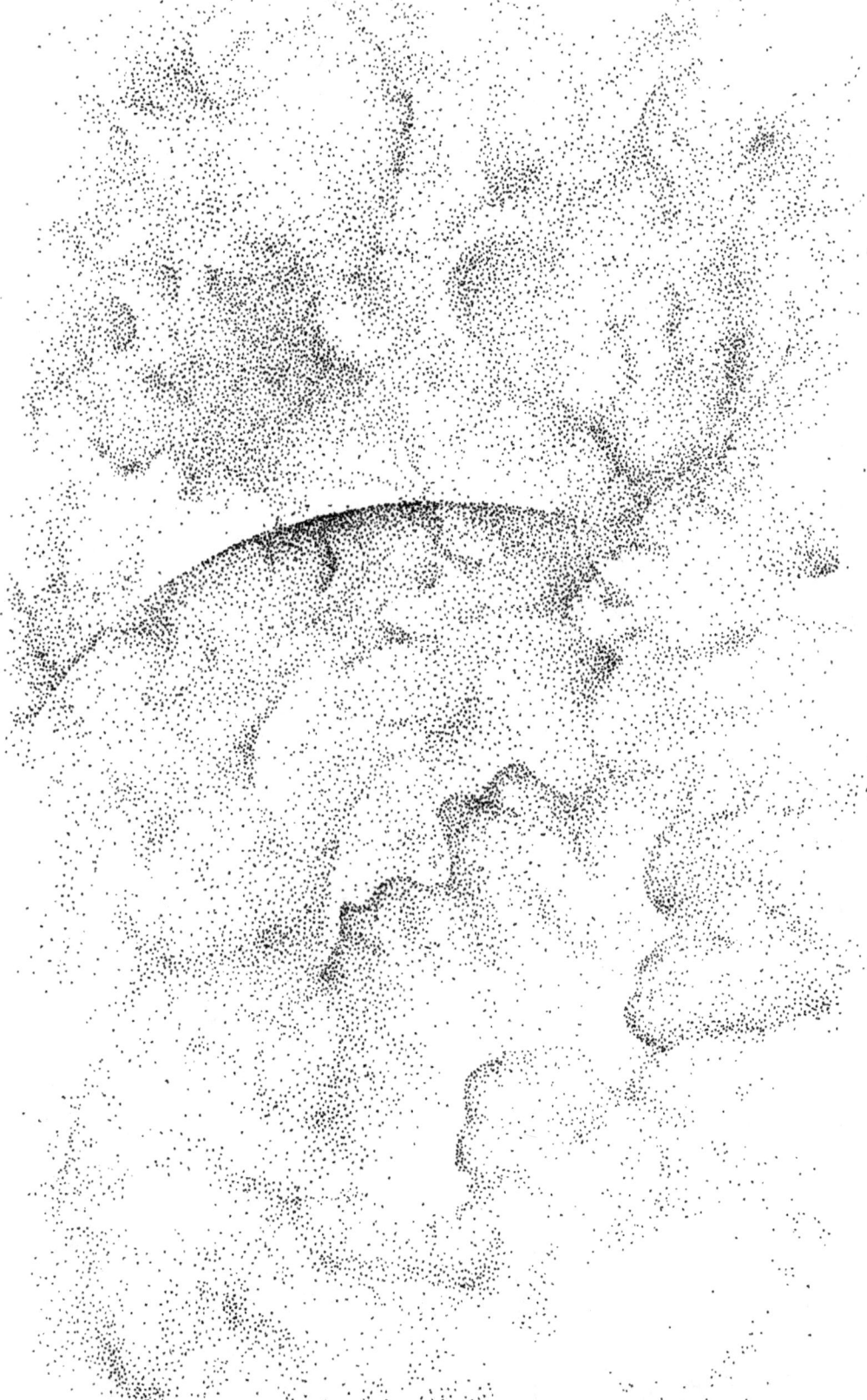

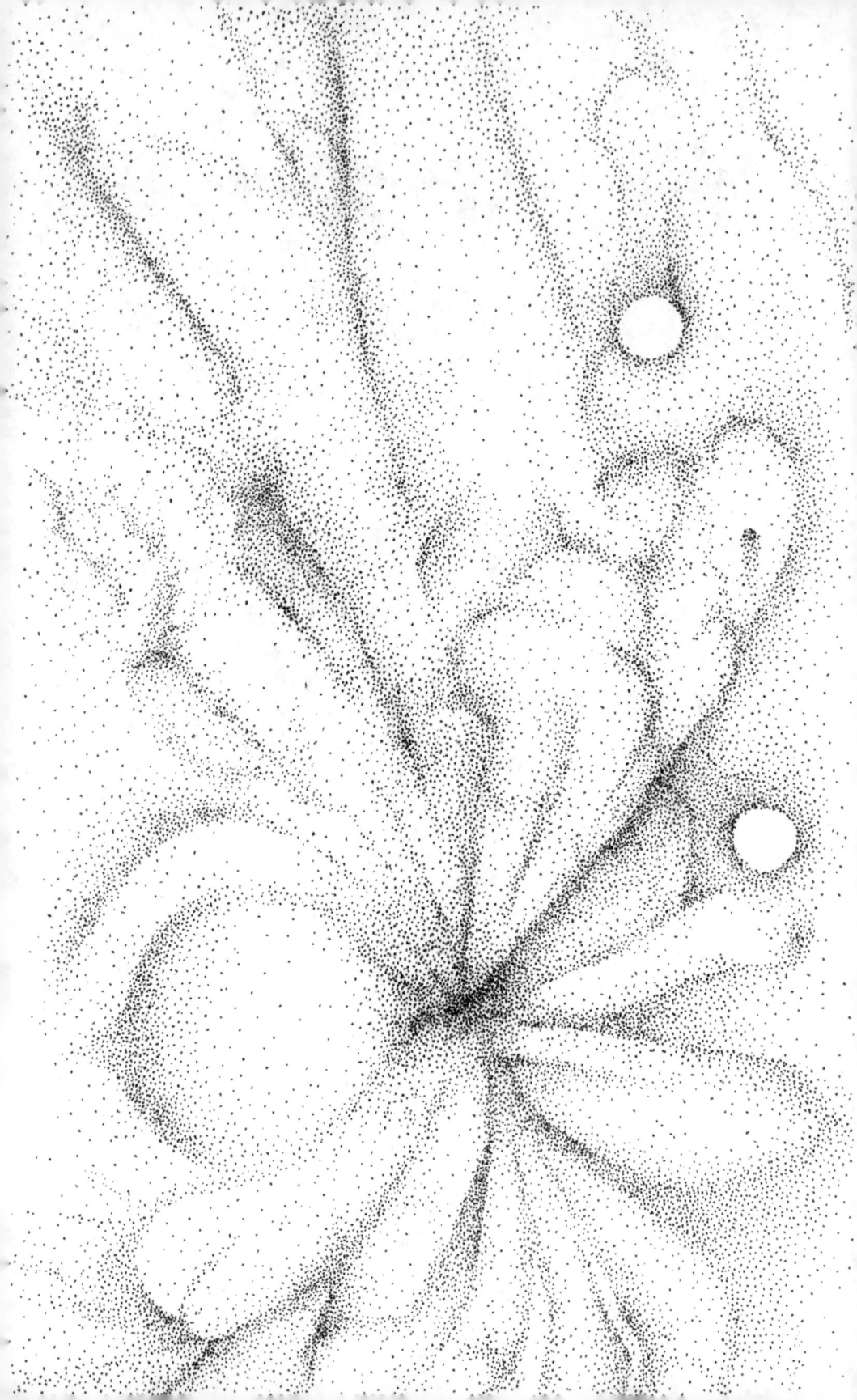

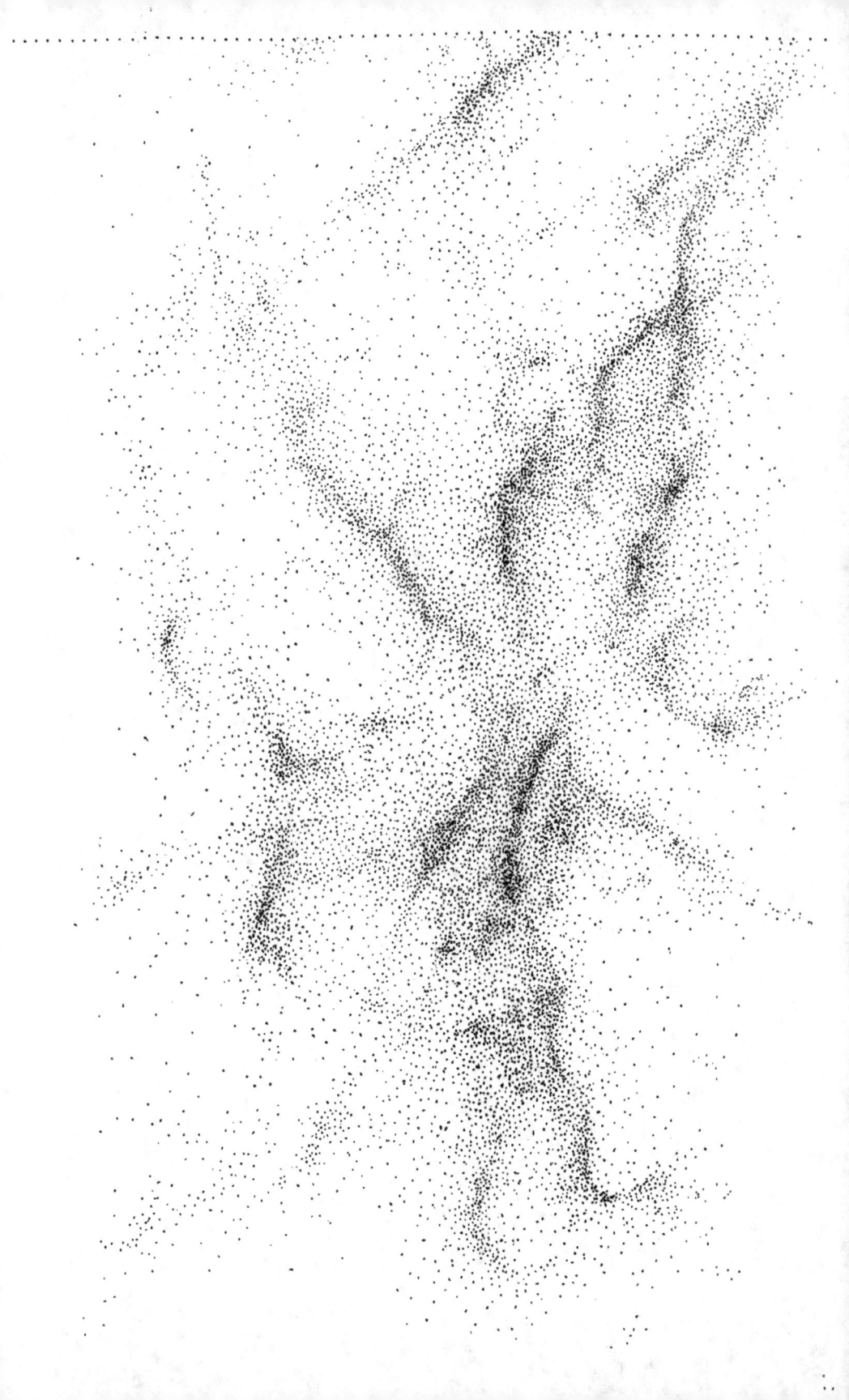

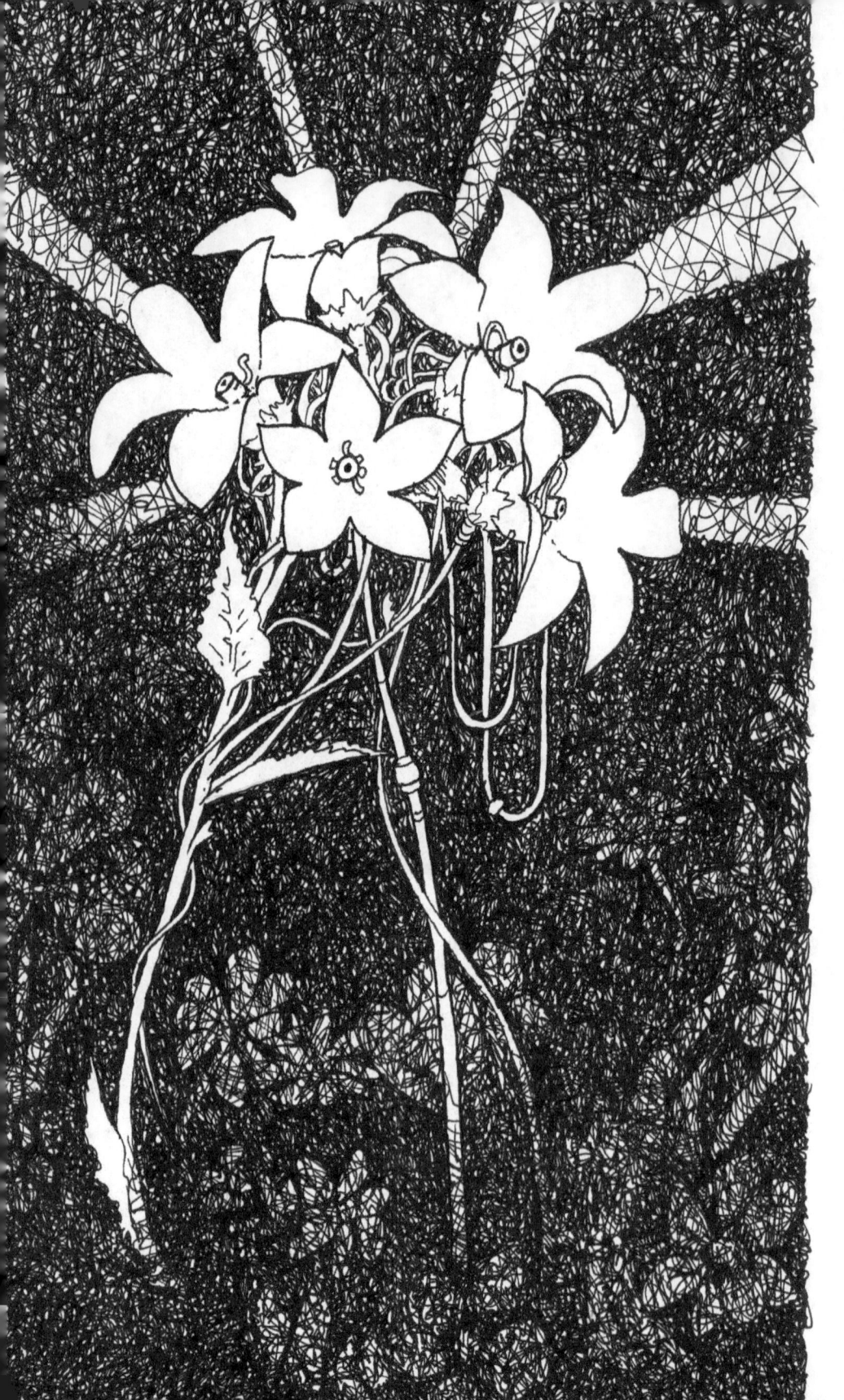

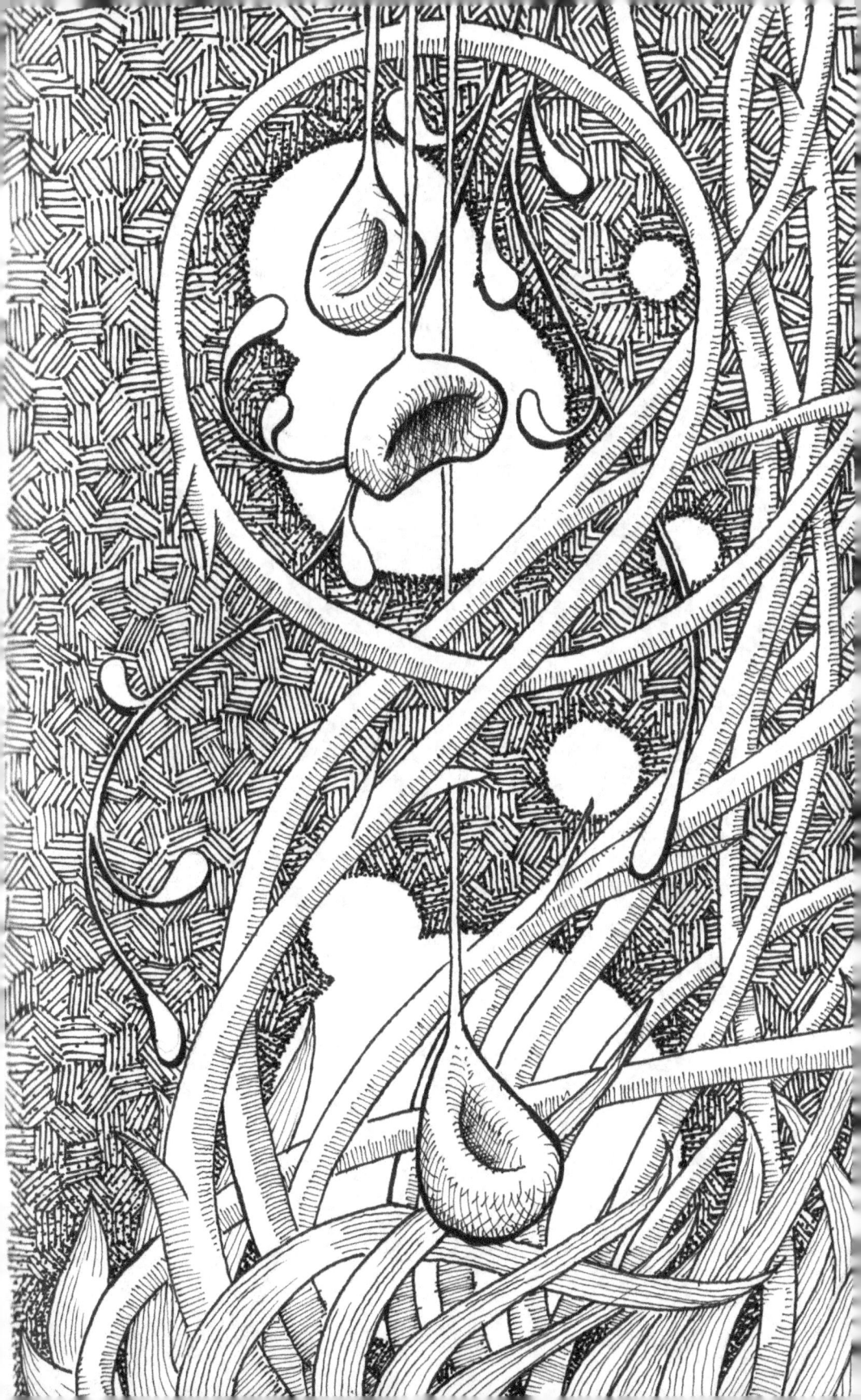

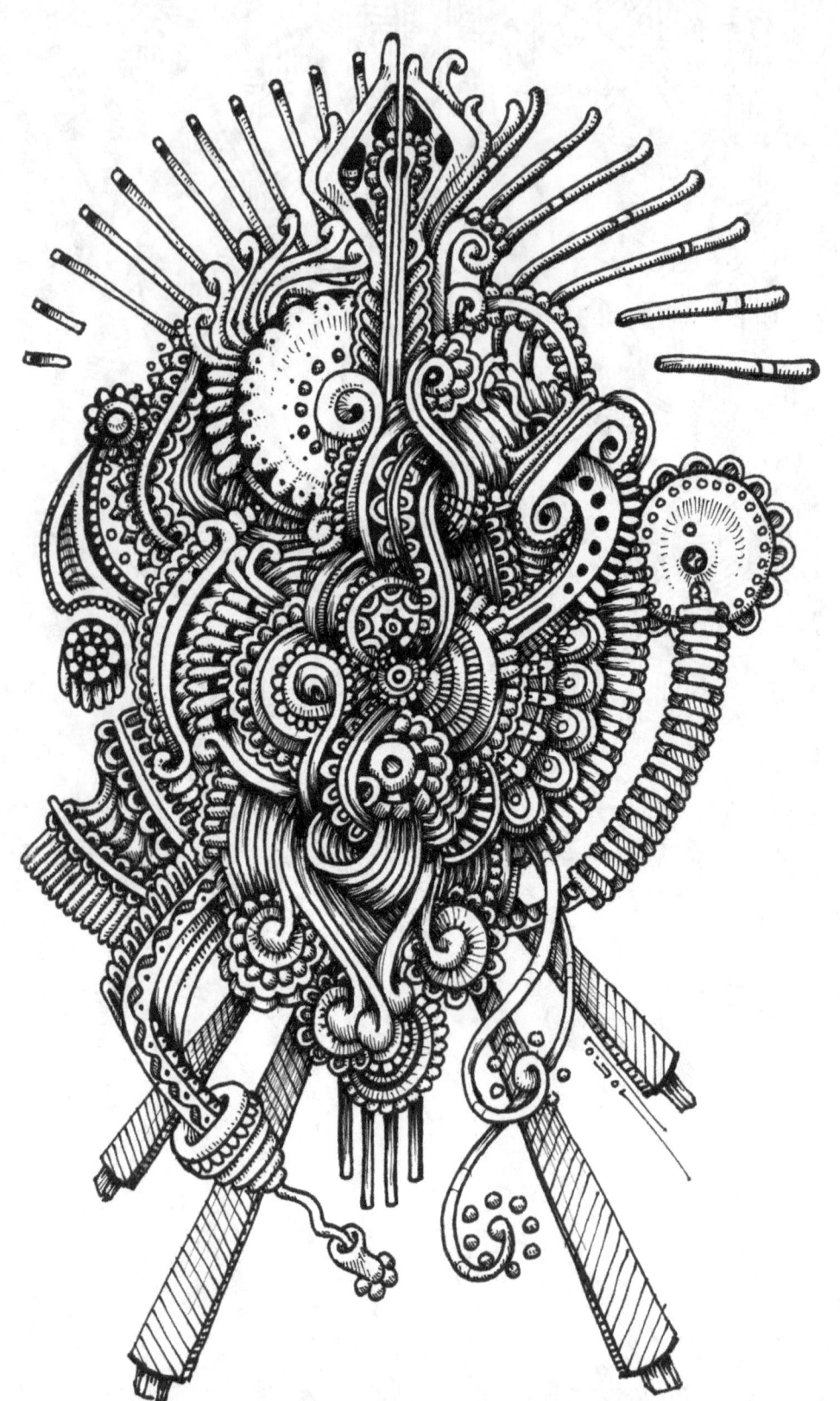

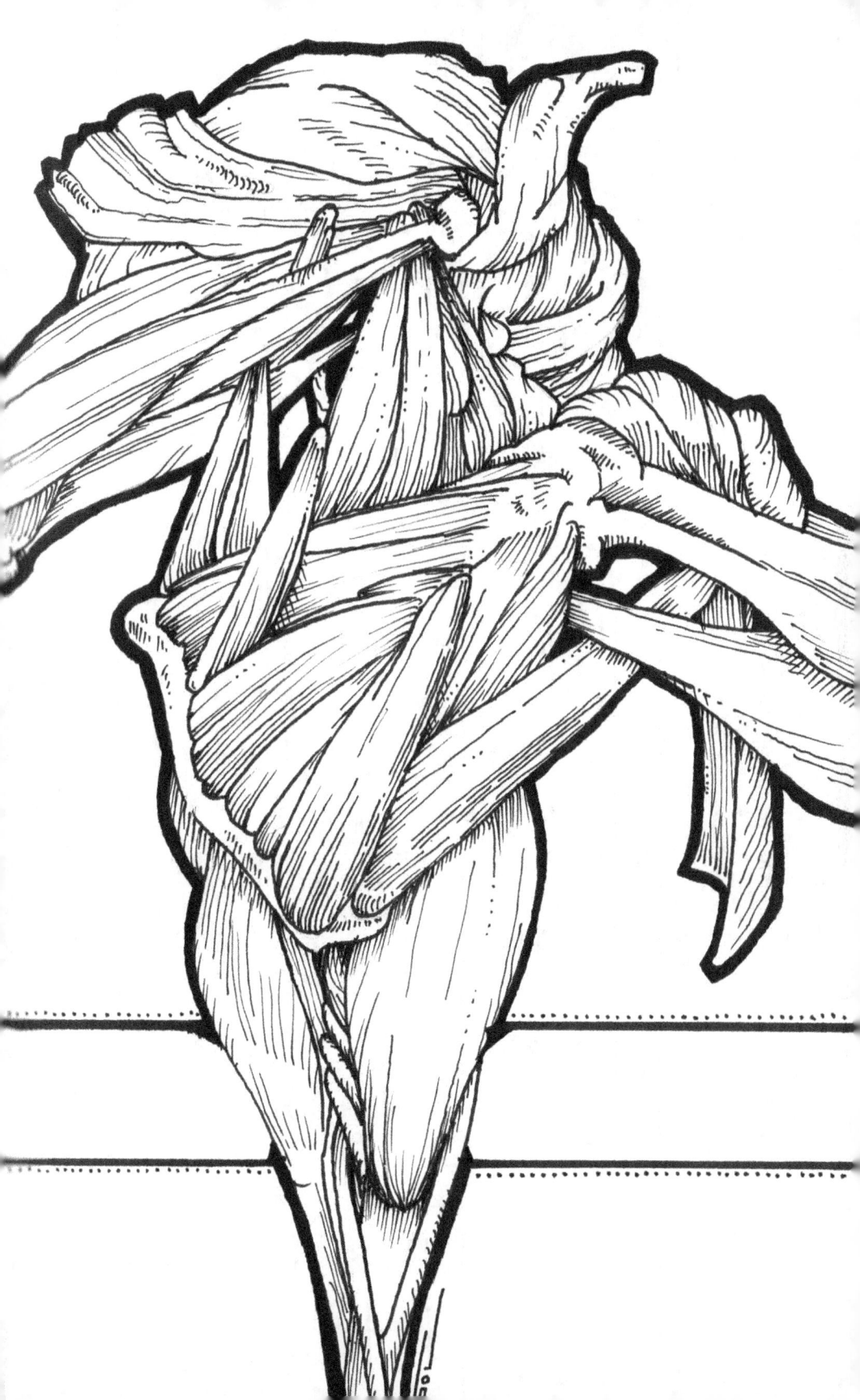

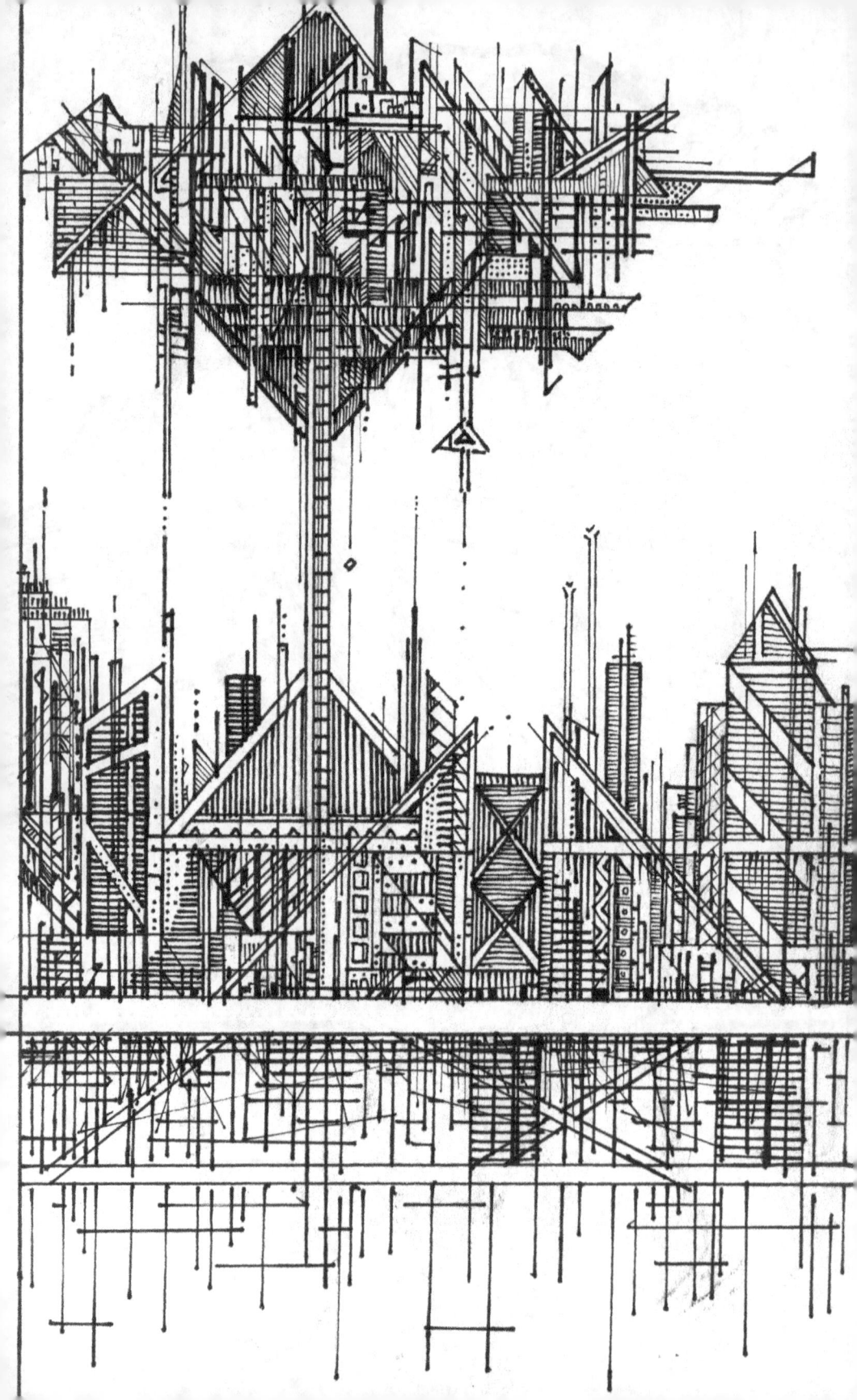

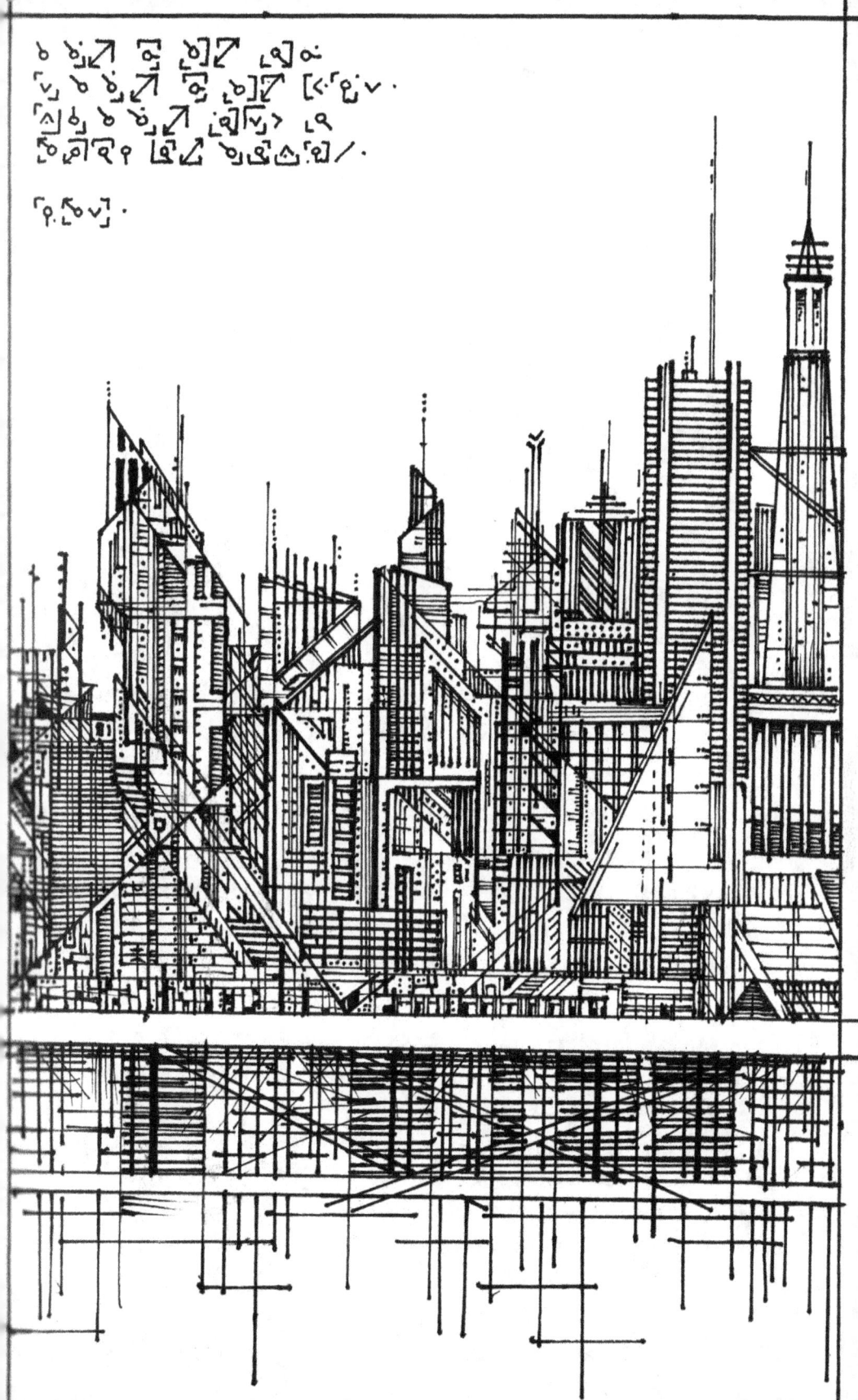

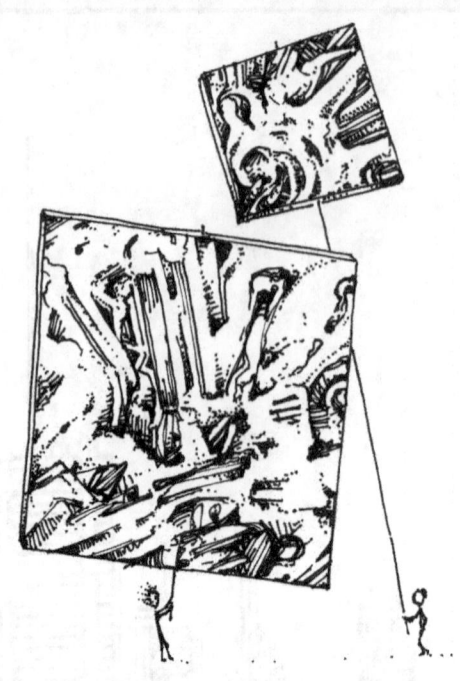

I expect the next big thing to be Pomelos. They are big, and a thing, and they are delicious. I'm not sure why more people don't know about them. They have alarmingly thick peels, almost a rind of sorts, to protect them from the more alarming horrors of the world around us. They have tiny oblong compartments of juice, similar to other citrus fruits like oranges and grapefruit; but amazingly each one of these little pockets of wonder will come apart on it's own to be fondled and eaten. It's all a truly broadening experience, and I would recommend to anyone with a functional mouth. It's like a pomegranate except you can't stain your clothes and there aren't hard seeds in the middle of each little pouch.

Now, I would like to take a moment to mention how great chairs are. When an individual engages in sitting in or upon one of these furnitary devices, the number of legs they have can effectively be increased by around 300%, which, I'm sure you can agree, is nothing to scoff at or brush aside. Chairs are "right up there" with pomelos.

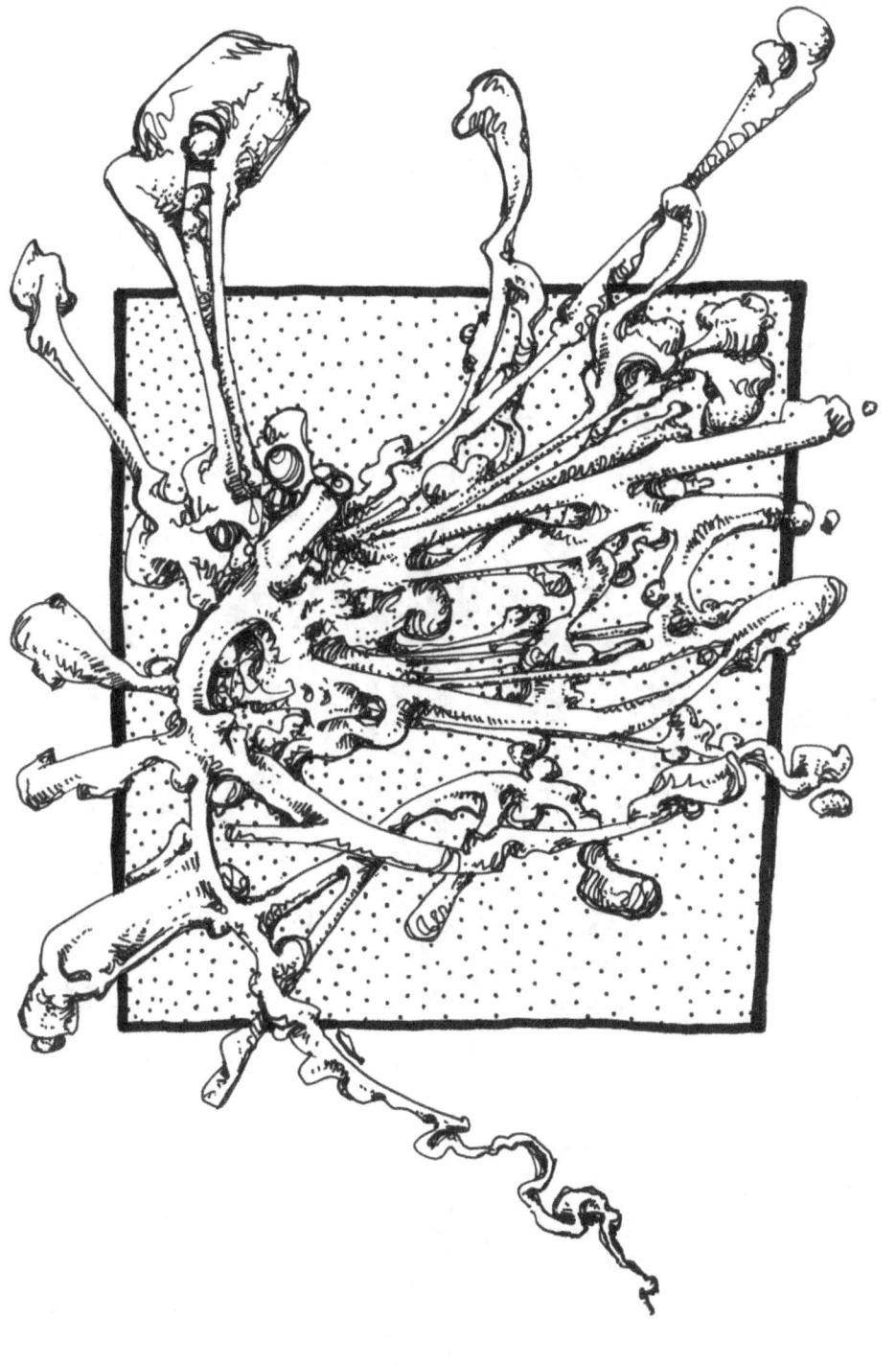

DIAGRAM OF A HOUSEBOAT

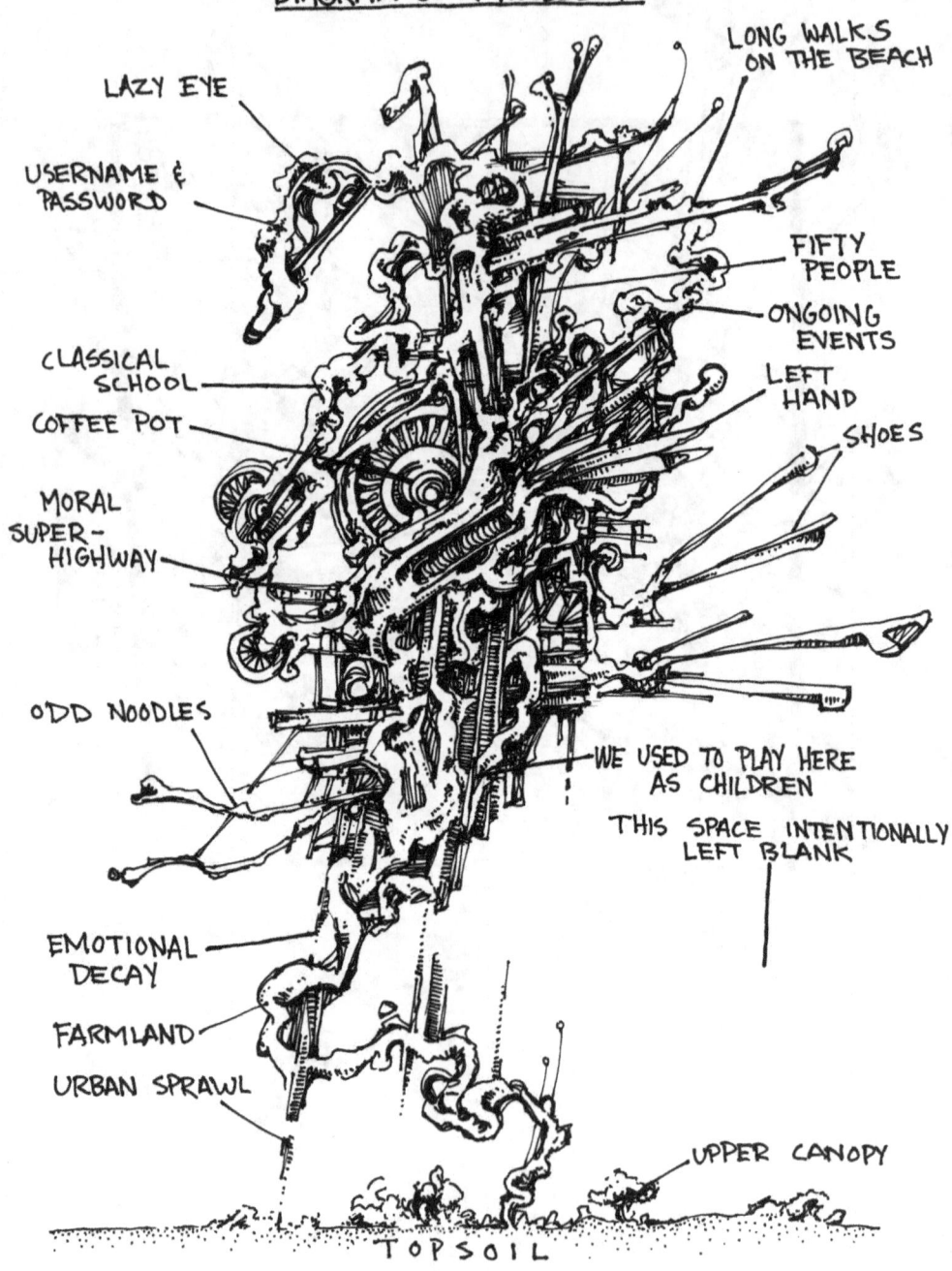

LONG WALKS
ON THE BEACH

LAZY EYE

USERNAME &
PASSWORD

FIFTY
PEOPLE

ONGOING
EVENTS

CLASSICAL
SCHOOL

LEFT
HAND

COFFEE POT

SHOES

MORAL
SUPER-
HIGHWAY

O'DD NOODLES

WE USED TO PLAY HERE
AS CHILDREN

THIS SPACE INTENTIONALLY
LEFT BLANK

EMOTIONAL
DECAY

FARMLAND

URBAN SPRAWL

UPPER CANOPY

TOPSOIL

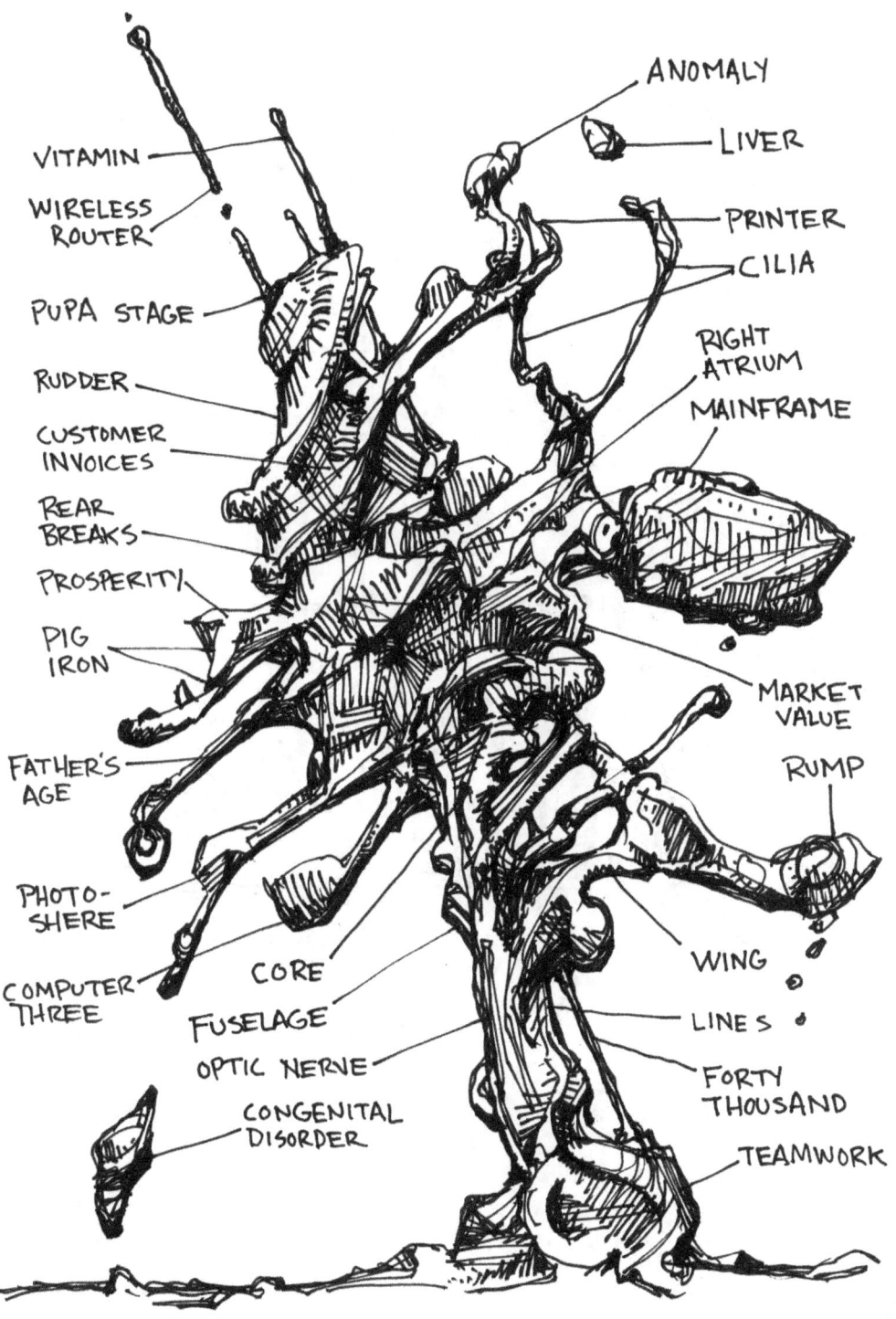

ANOMALY

LIVER

VITAMIN

WIRELESS
ROUTER

PRINTER

CILIA

PUPA STAGE

RIGHT
ATRIUM

RUDDER

MAINFRAME

CUSTOMER
INVOICES

REAR
BREAKS

PROSPERITY

PIG
IRON

MARKET
VALUE

FATHER'S
AGE

RUMP

PHOTO-
SHERE

CORE

COMPUTER
THREE

FUSELAGE

WING

OPTIC NERVE

LINES

CONGENITAL
DISORDER

FORTY
THOUSAND

TEAMWORK

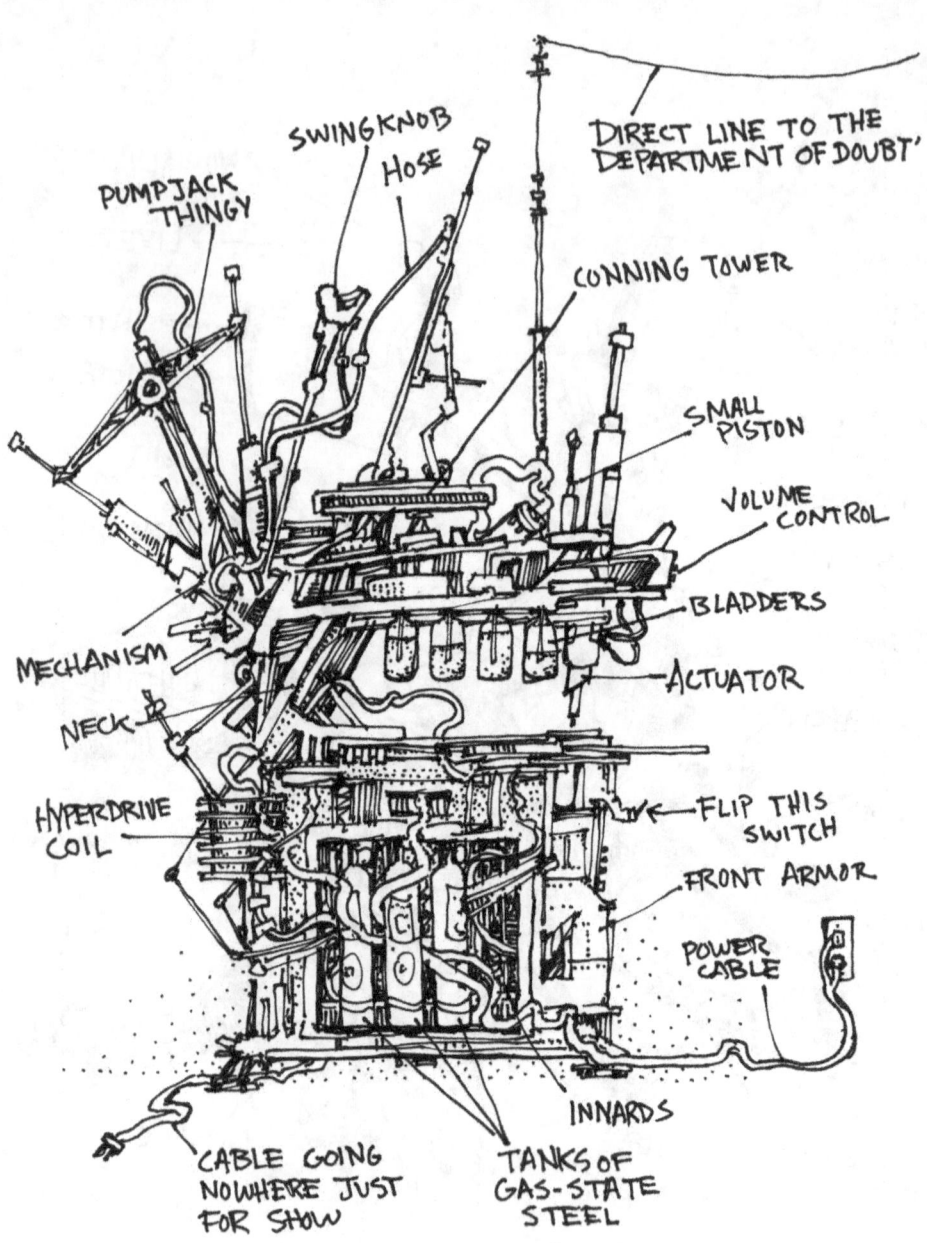

PUMPJACK THINGY

SWINGKNOB

HOSE

DIRECT LINE TO THE DEPARTMENT OF DOUBT'

CONNING TOWER

SMALL PISTON

VOLUME CONTROL

BLADDERS

ACTUATOR

MECHANISM

NECK

FLIP THIS SWITCH

HYPERDRIVE COIL

FRONT ARMOR

POWER CABLE

INNARDS

CABLE GOING NOWHERE JUST FOR SHOW

TANKS OF GAS-STATE STEEL

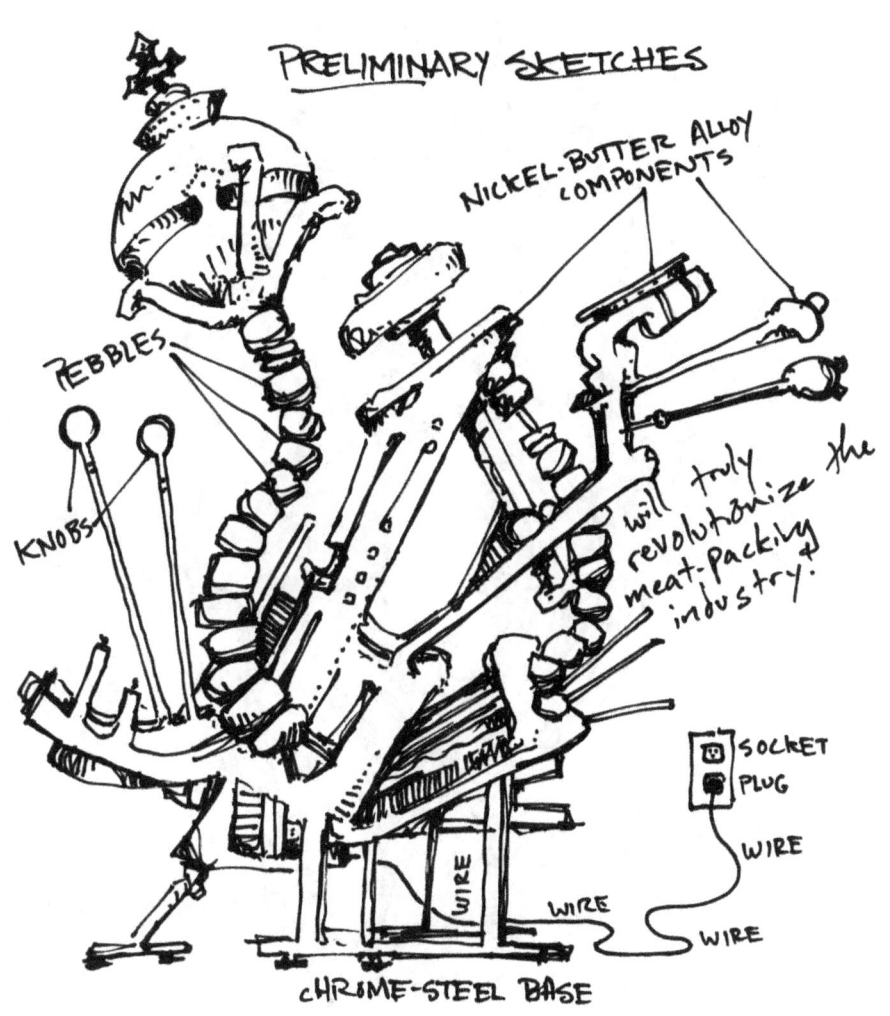

PRELIMINARY SKETCHES

NICKEL-BUTTER ALLOY
COMPONENTS

PEBBLES

KNOBS

will truly
revolutionize the
meat-packing
industry.

SOCKET
PLUG

WIRE

WIRE

WIRE

WIRE

CHROME-STEEL BASE

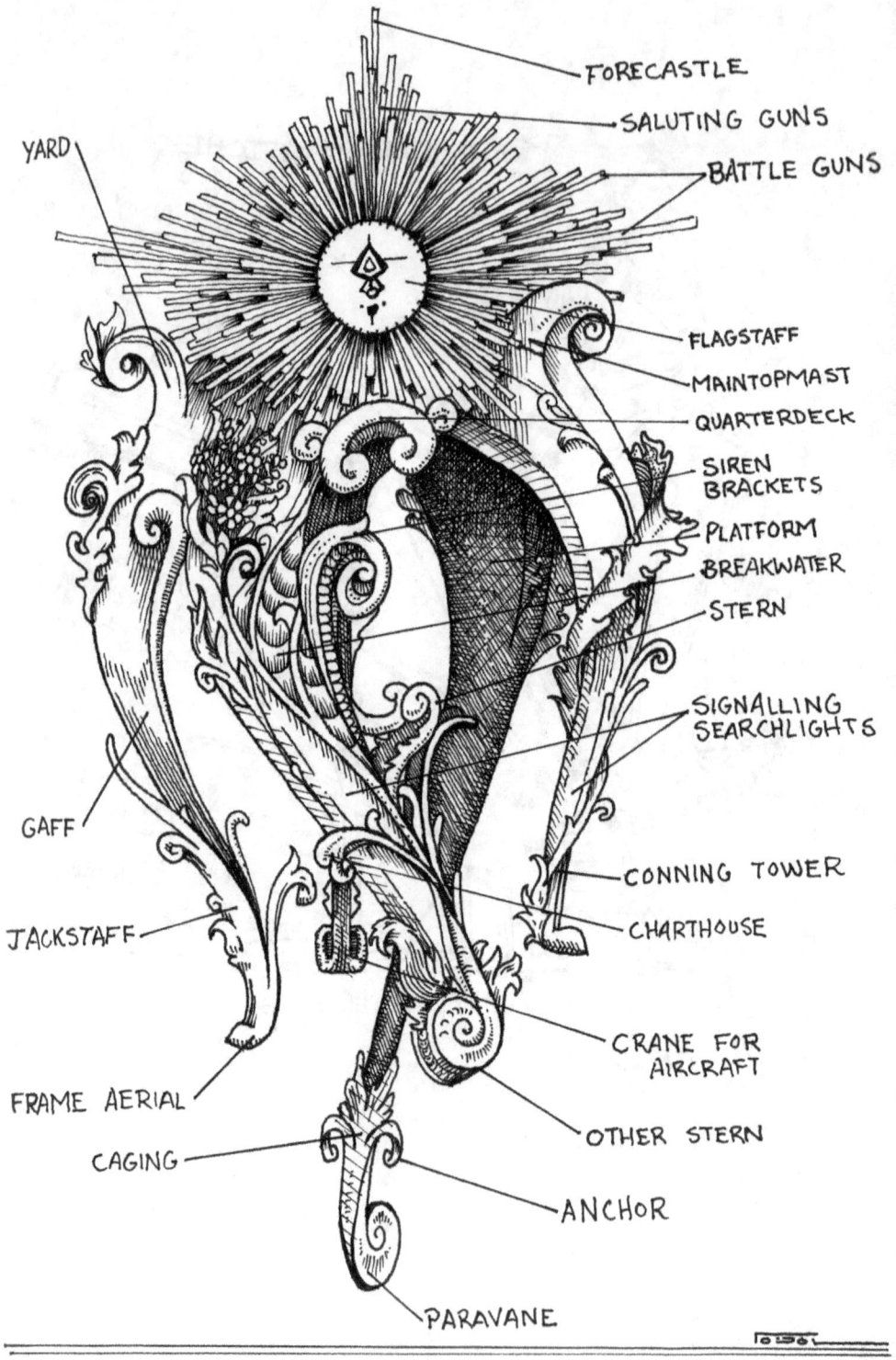

FORECASTLE

SALUTING GUNS

BATTLE GUNS

YARD

FLAGSTAFF

MAINTOPMAST

QUARTERDECK

SIREN
BRACKETS

PLATFORM

BREAKWATER

STERN

SIGNALLING
SEARCHLIGHTS

GAFF

JACKSTAFF

CONNING TOWER

CHARTHOUSE

FRAME AERIAL

CRANE FOR
AIRCRAFT

CAGING

OTHER STERN

ANCHOR

PARAVANE

∾

∘ LEARNING ABOUT THE ∘
BATTLESHIP.

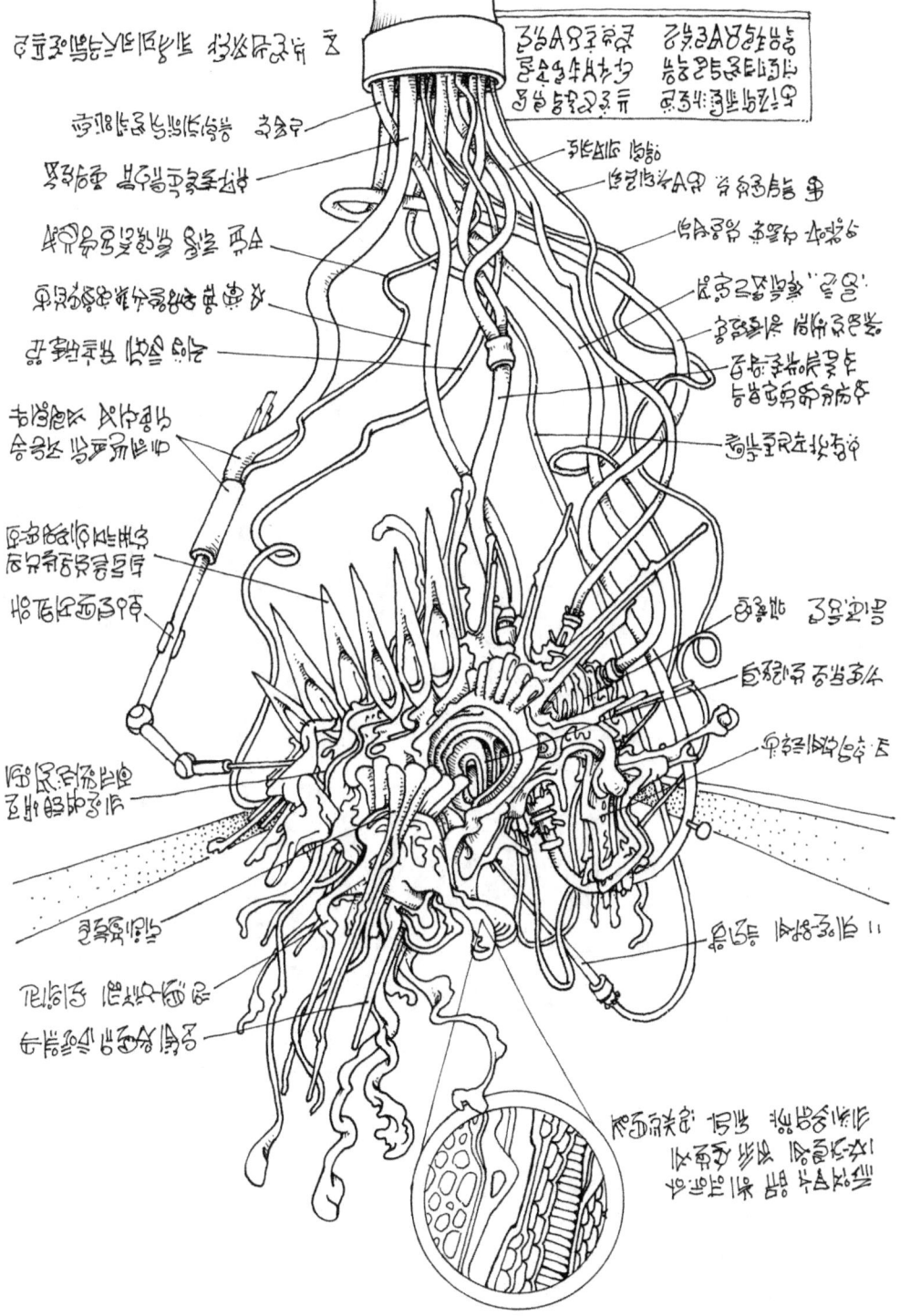

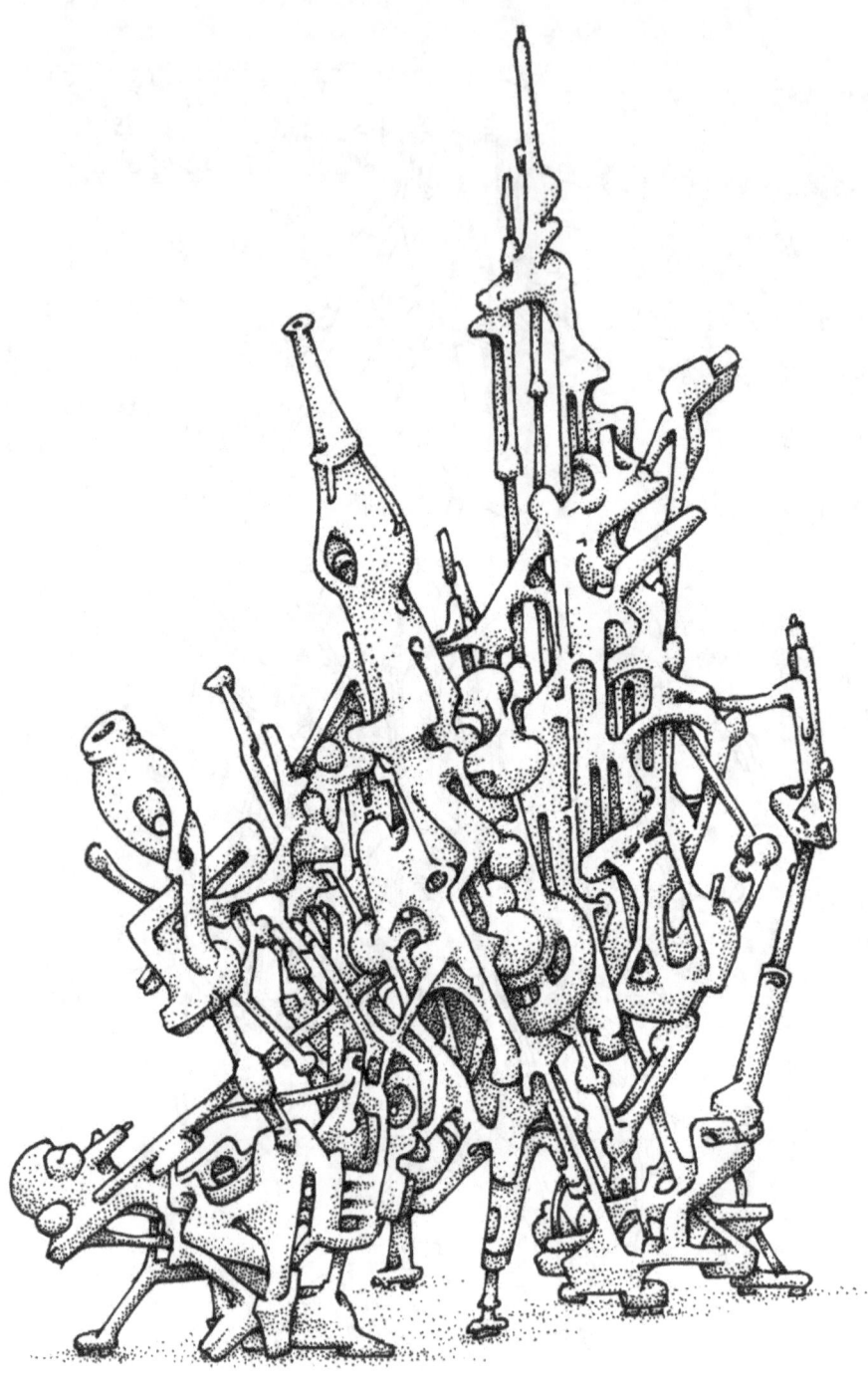

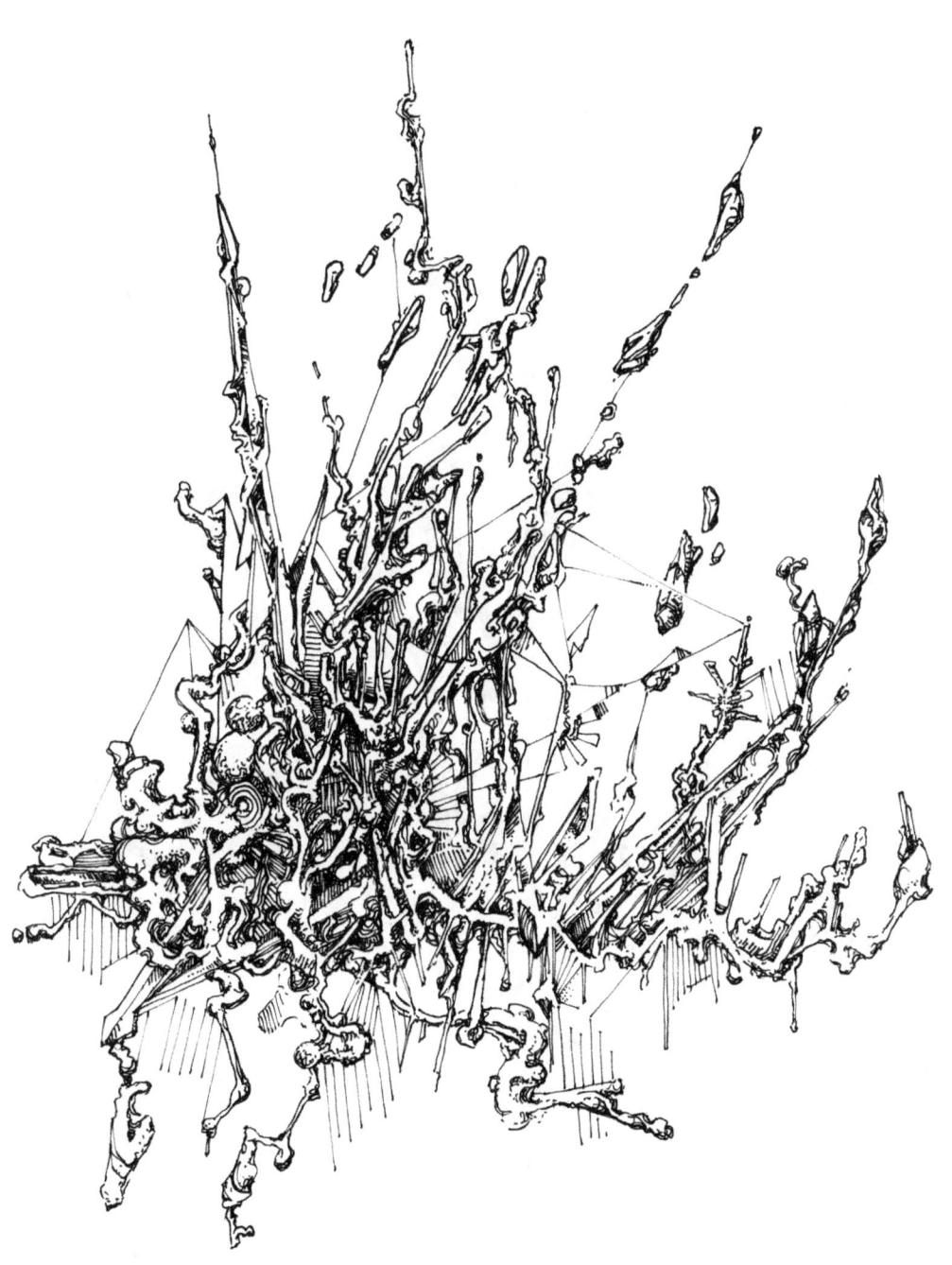

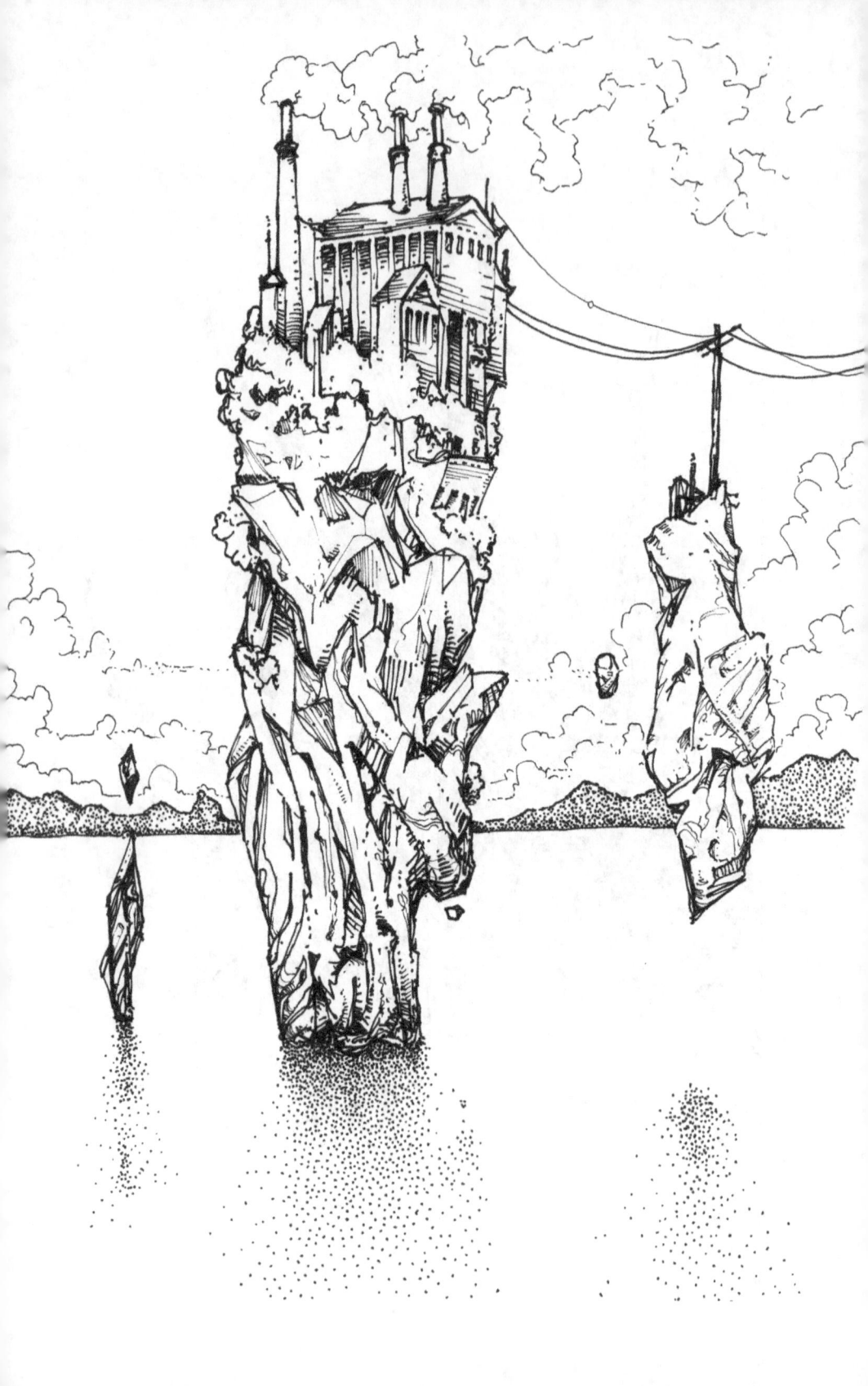

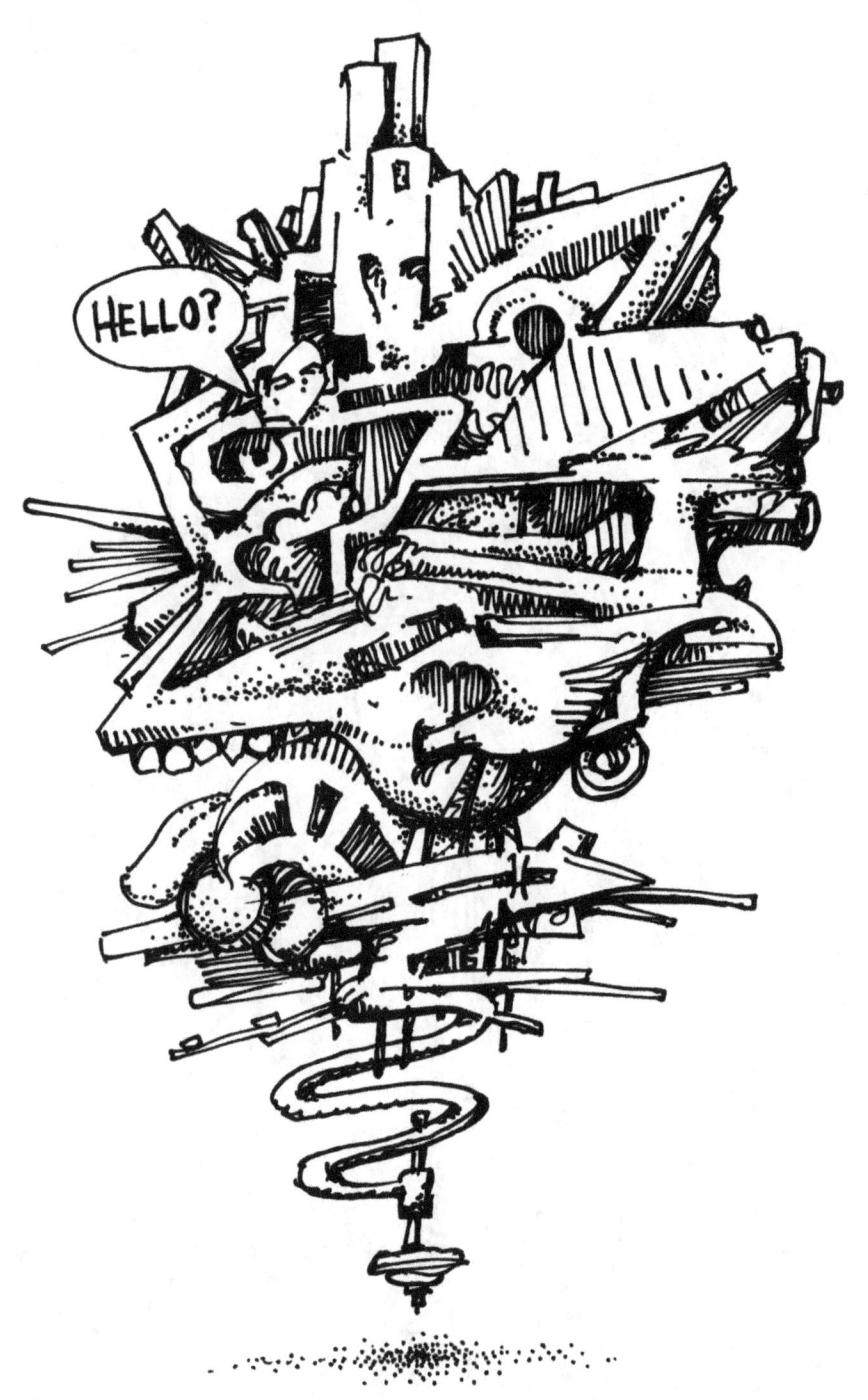

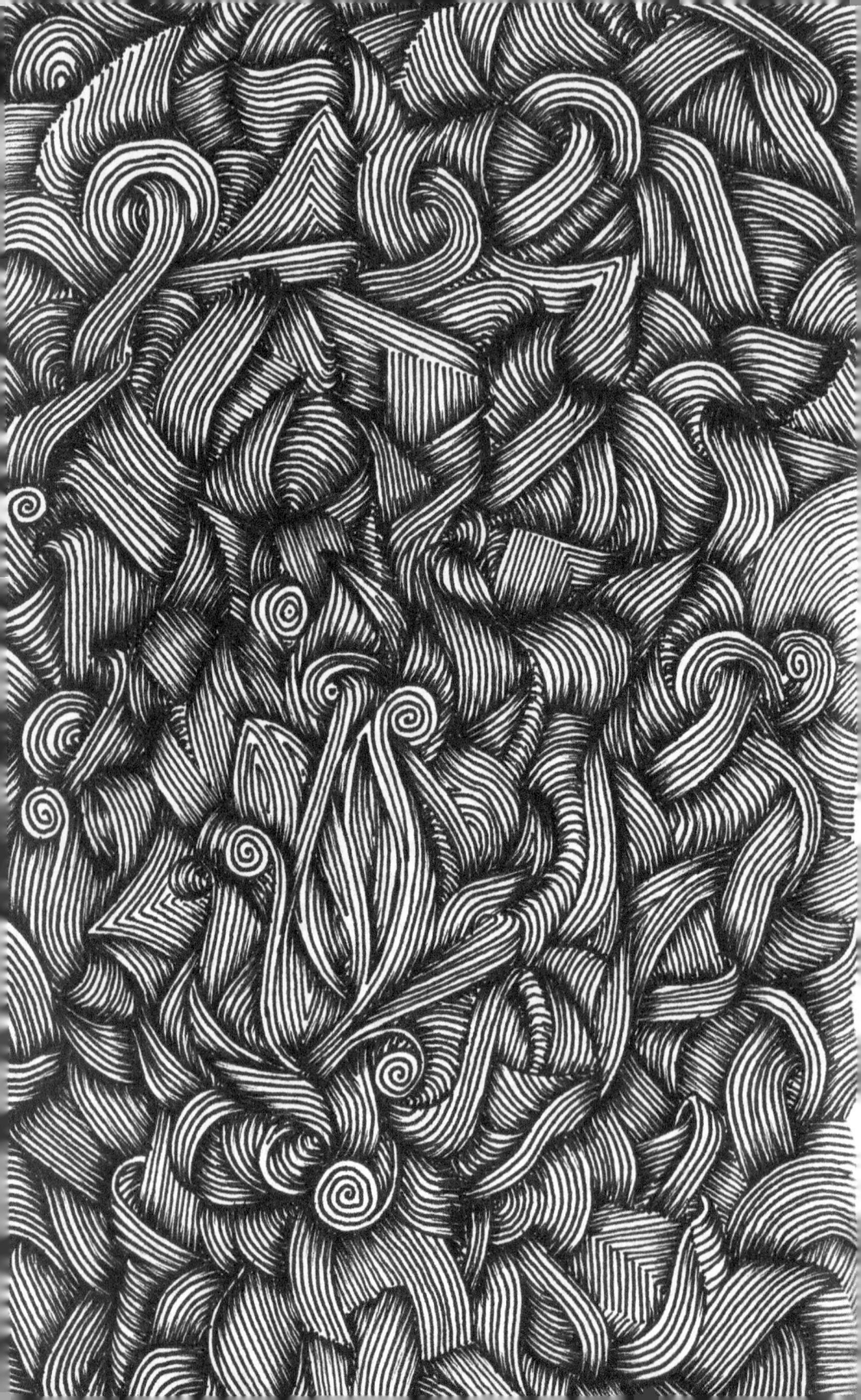

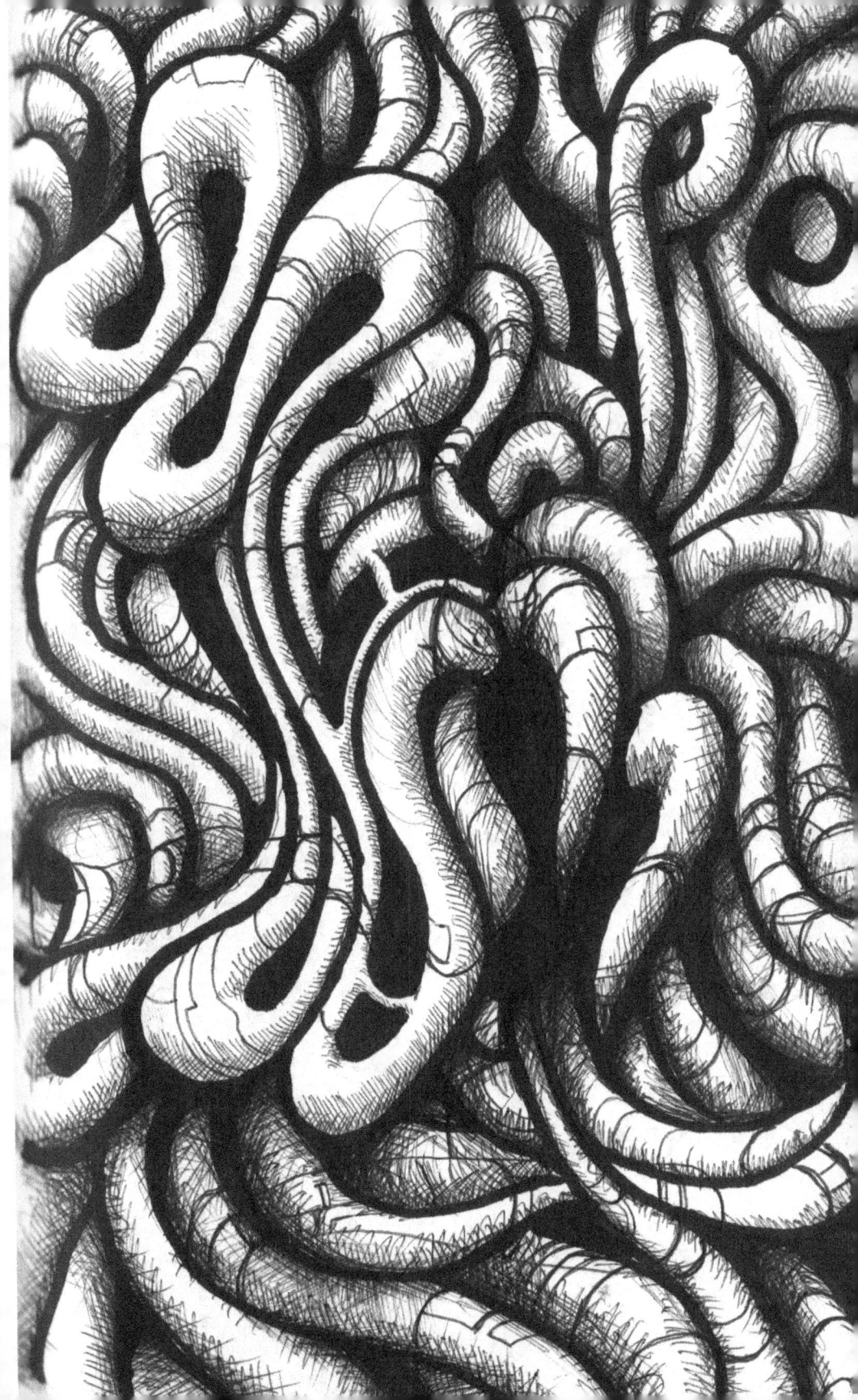

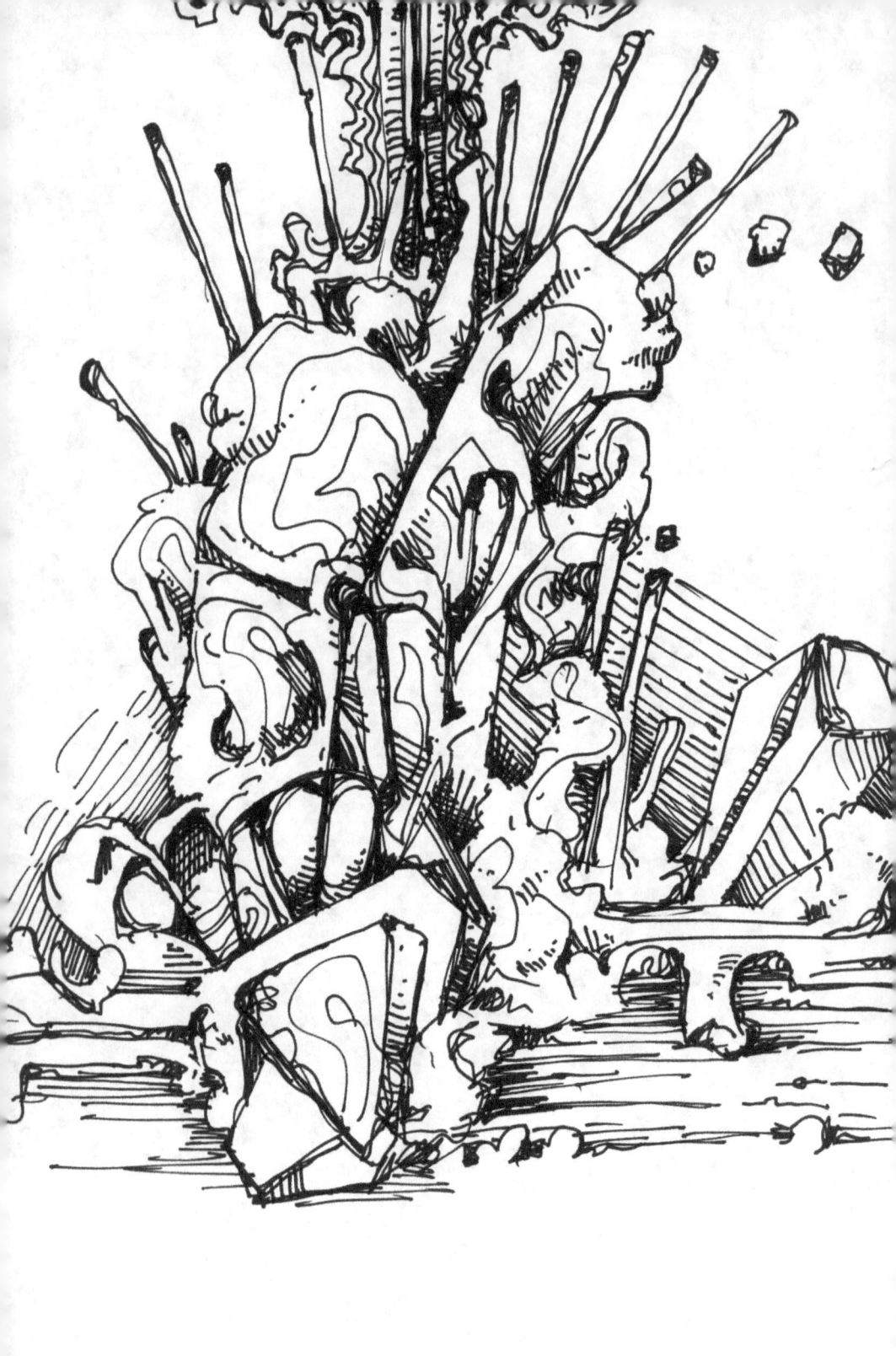

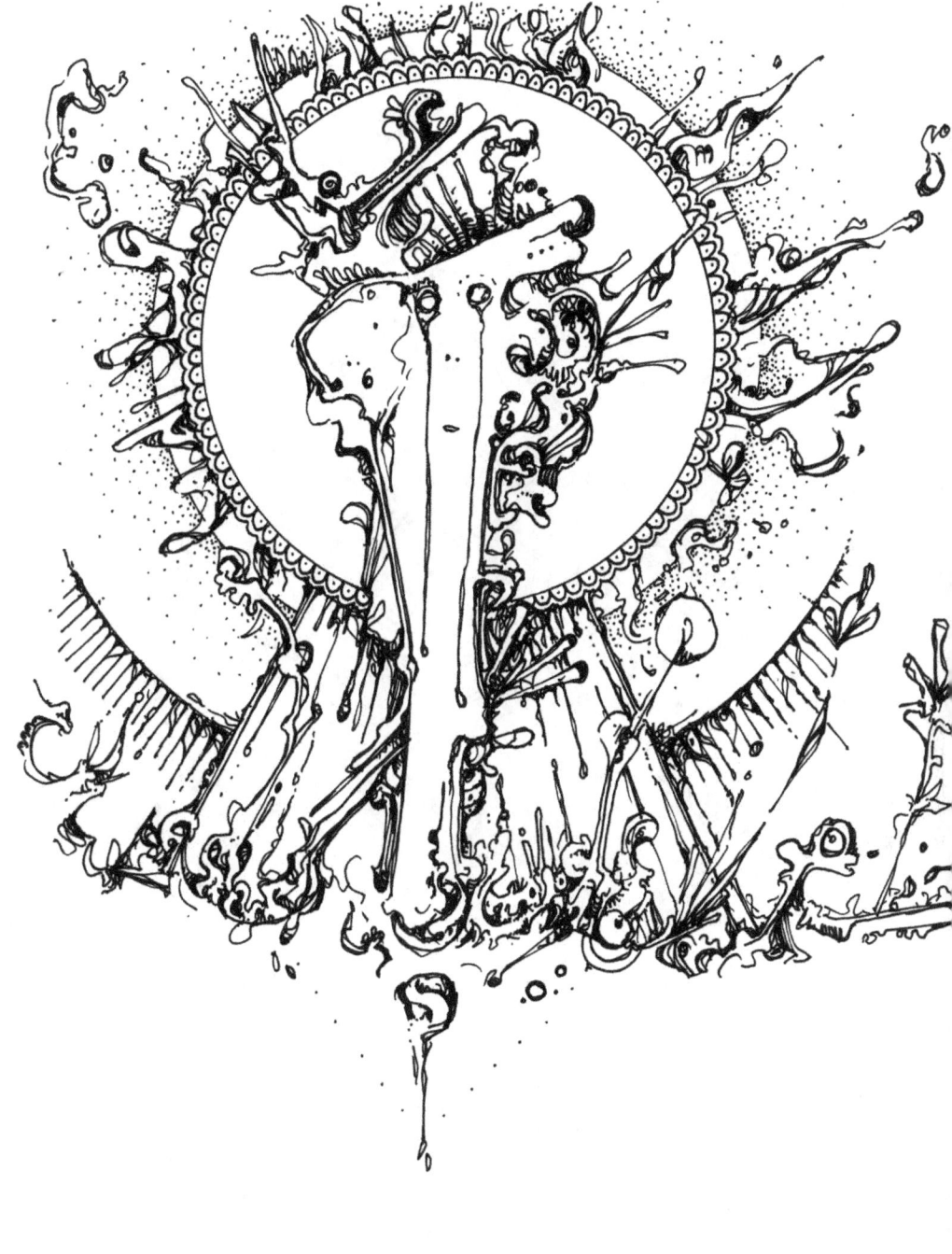

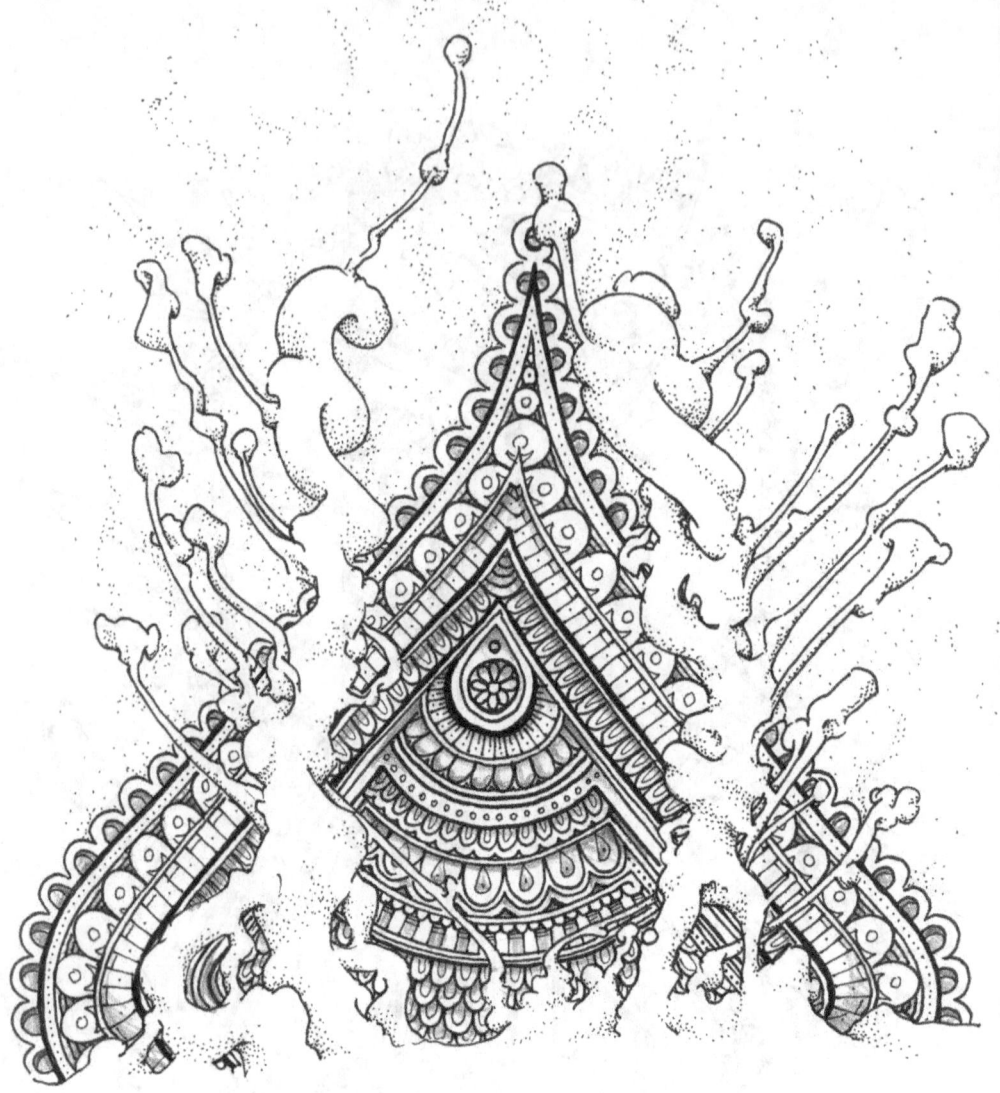

It's difficult to predict what you're getting yourself into when you commit to a banana. On the other hand, perhaps I'm an amateur. Many a time I have peeled open a banana with <u>plenty</u> of scarring and scrapes on the outside only for it to be close to perfectly unscathed on the inside, and other times I've peeled a perfect-looking one with eager anticipation only to be greeted by a mottled, bruised mess of a fruit. All bananas have seeds, but most of the ones we eat these days have seeds so small they don't bother us. When we ate ones with bigger, noticeable seeds, we called those monkey bananas.

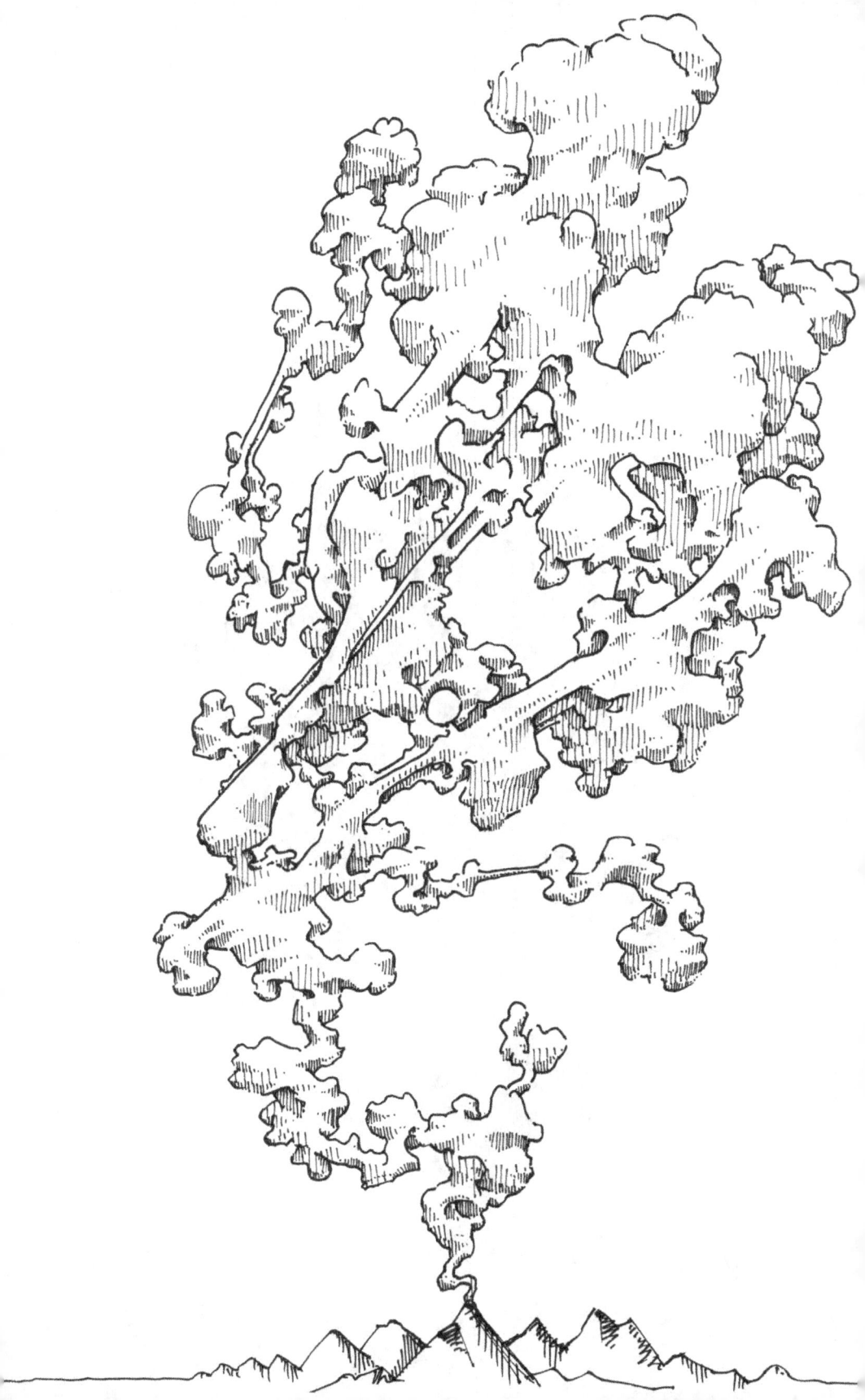

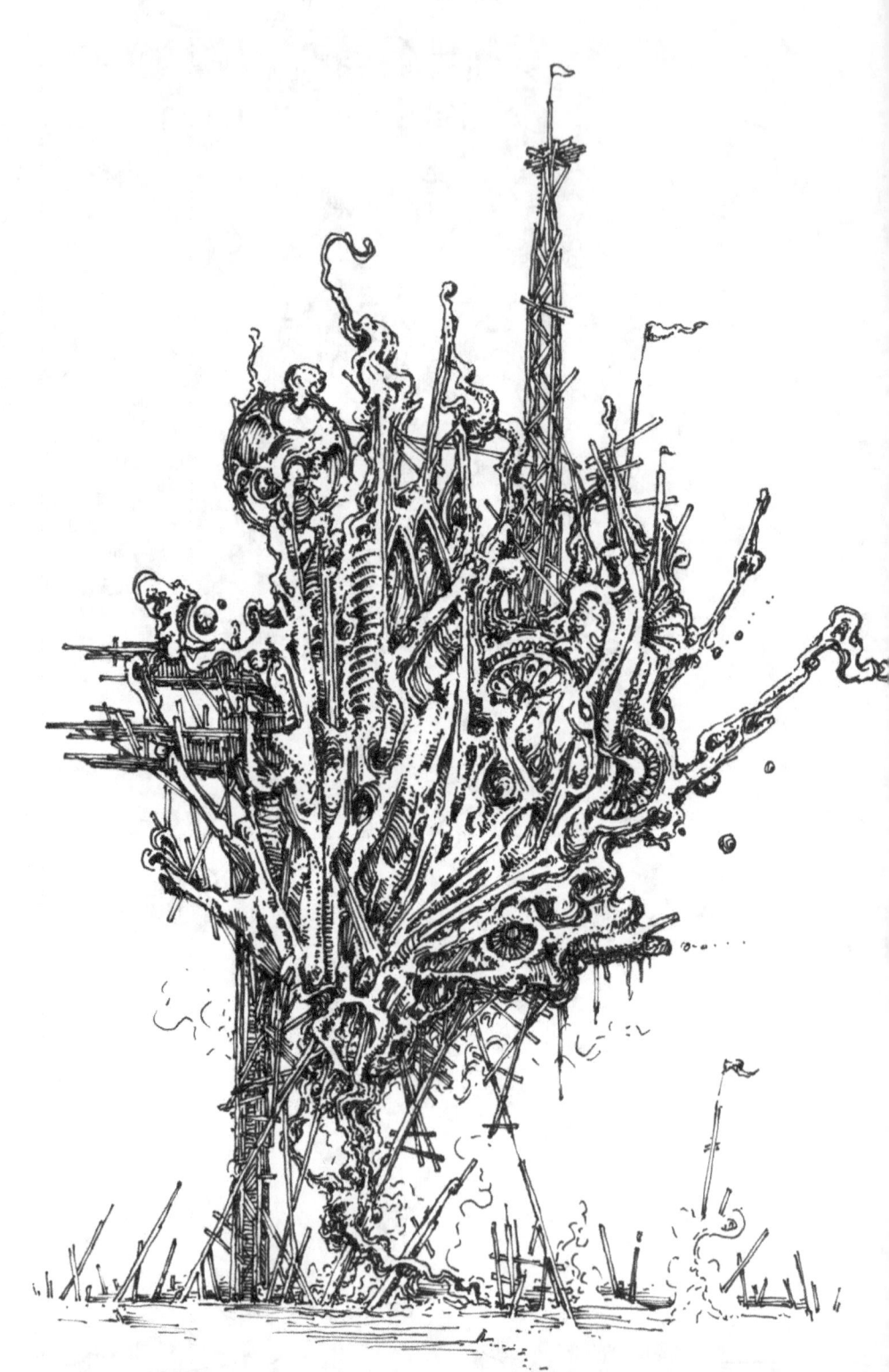

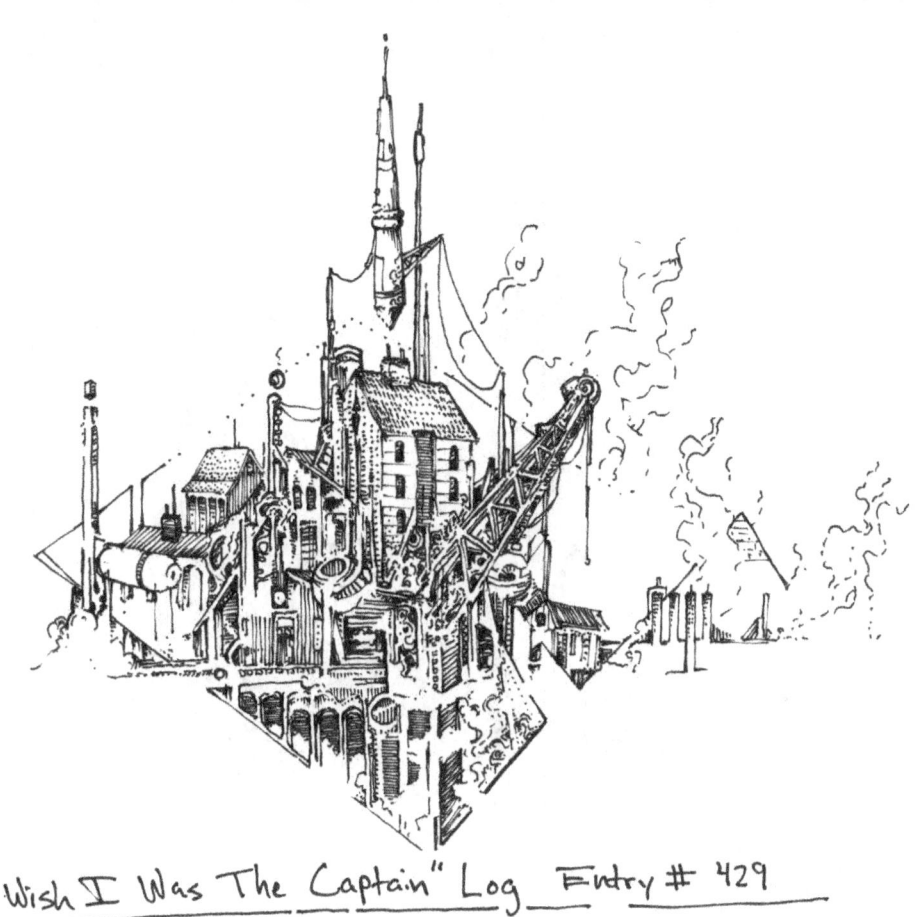

"I Wish I Was The Captain" Log   Entry # 429

It's been, on this day, exactly 16 years since
I left my home and family and embarked on
this voyage to find that one island people
were telling all those terribly fantastic tales
about. Needless to say we didn't find it and
like many other stories you might've heard
we found ourselves quickly marooned on an
entirely separate small island ever since then.
Things haven't been entirely abysmal, however.
I have opened a semi-successful stock brokerage
firm, which I hardly know anything about,
but it's been great to learn as I go. Half
the battle has been convincing some of the
other seven survivors that they need my services
to be personally and financially successful. An
uphill battle on an almost entirely uninhabited
island, but I sure have learned a lot.

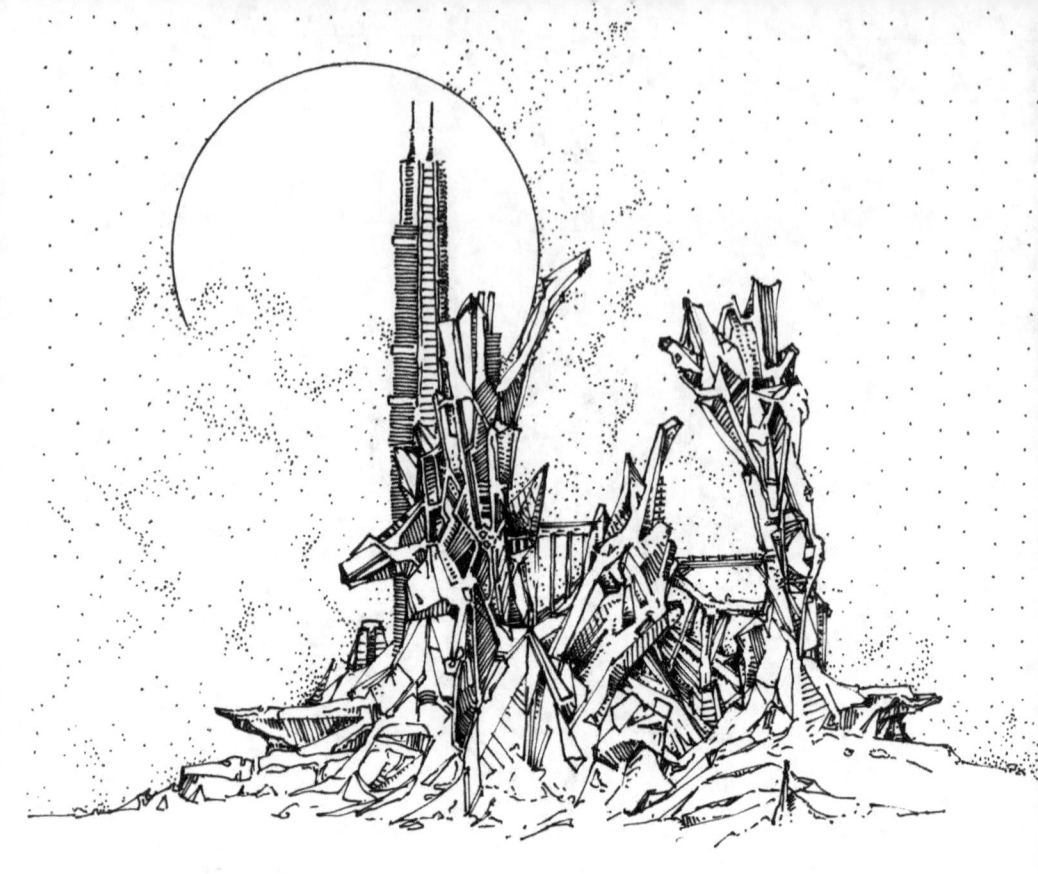

Sometimes I think back to my wife and 5-year-old son (he must have grown older by now. I'm not sure) and I wonder If they've also followed in my footsteps and opened their own stock-brokerage firms. Somehow I think this is a little unrealistic since they have so many regulations and certifications and various other hurdles to crawl over headfirst over there in the States, and I simply created all these regulatory agencies for myself and then disregarded them here on the island. Hopefully they don't catch on for a while. Anyways, It's fun to think about.

THE FIVE & A HALF SHISH KEBABS of TRUE HUNGER

An appropriate and rigorous consumption of The Kebabs yields nifty results.

SIMPLICITY   DEPLORABILITY   IMMEDIATELY   AMPHIBOLY   APOLOGY   MEMORY

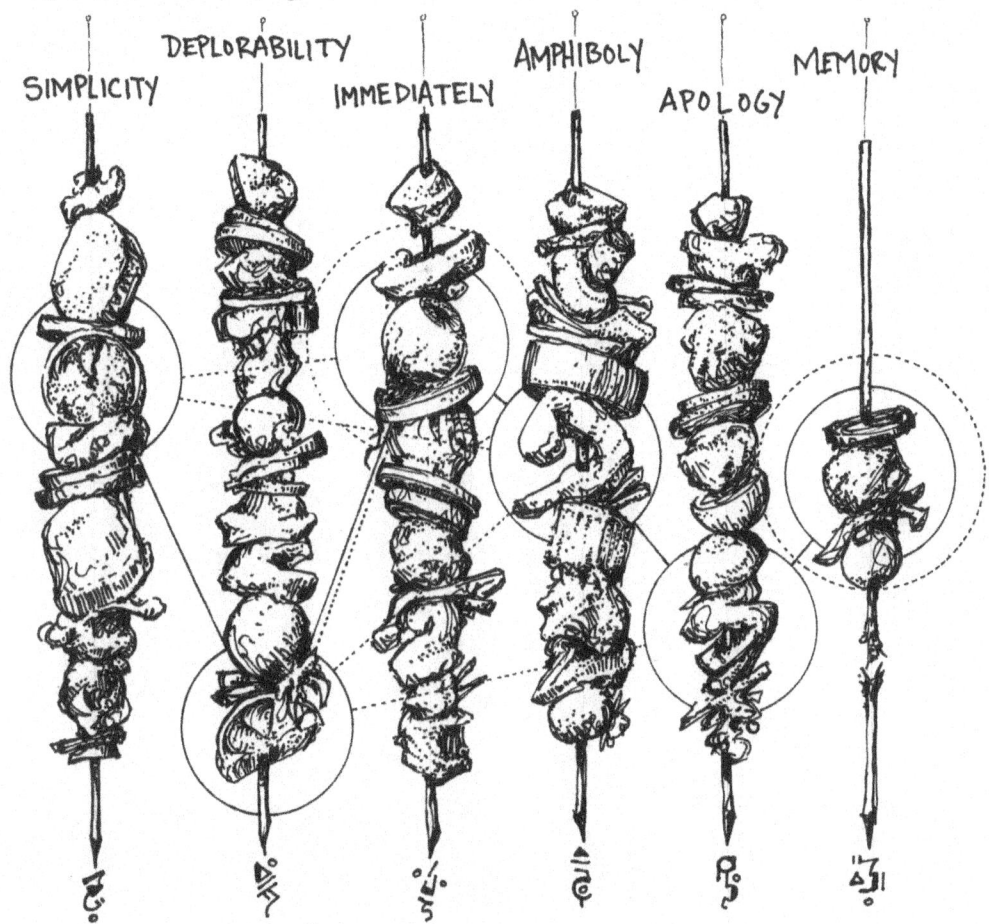

IT WASN'T UNTIL LATE IN THE '40s WHEN THE FIRST
KEBAB WAS UNEARTHED IN VERMONT BY A HOUSEWIFE
DIGGING WITH A TROWEL IN HER YARD IN A FOOLISH
ATTEMPT TO GROW BEGONIAS WHEN THE WHOLE
CONCEPT BEGAN TO TAKE FORM AND EMERGE FROM
MYTH INTO SOMETHING THAT WOULD REALLY PROMOTE
THE SALE OF DECORATIVE SKEWERS AND SMALL
PORCELAIN GRILLS FOR PEOPLE TO ROAST THEIR WHIMS
AND WILLS AND MENTAL PRAWNS UPON IN A CLOUDED
EFFORT TO SLAKE THE THIRST LEFT BEHIND BY
EVERYTHING THEY HAD BEEN EATING THAT
HADN'T BEEN ONE OR MORE OF THE
FIVE & A HALF SHISH KEBABS of TRUE HUNGER

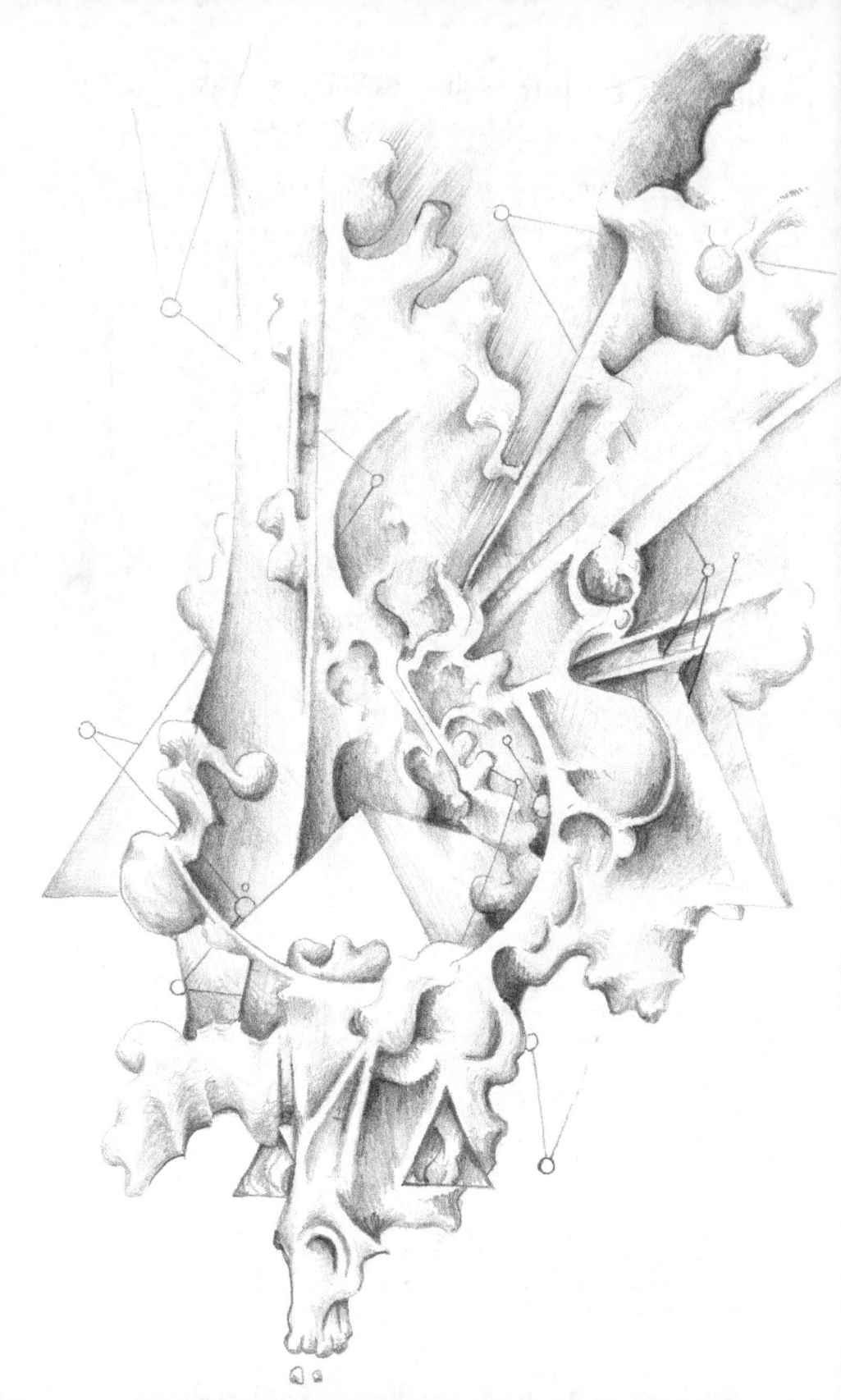

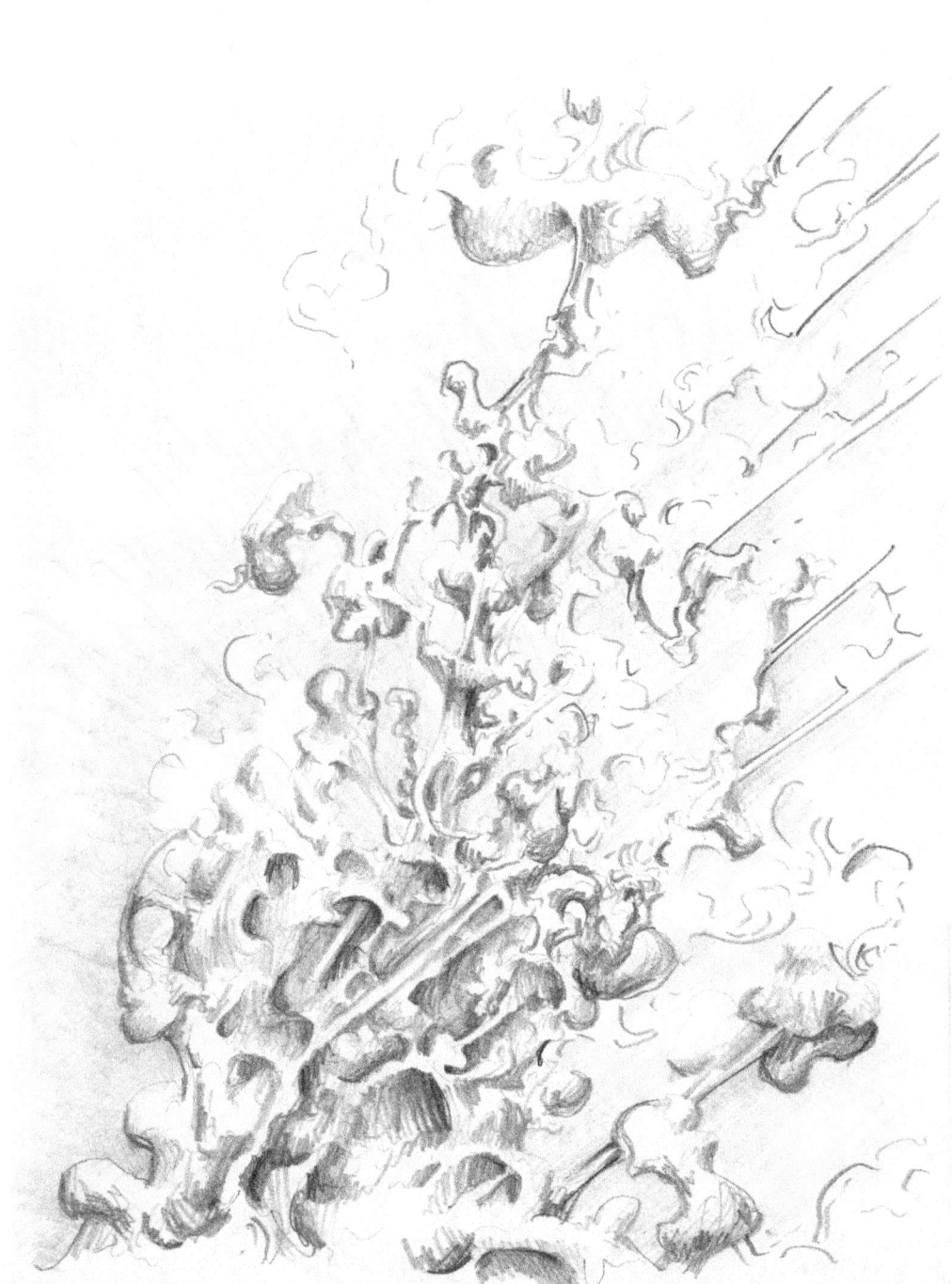

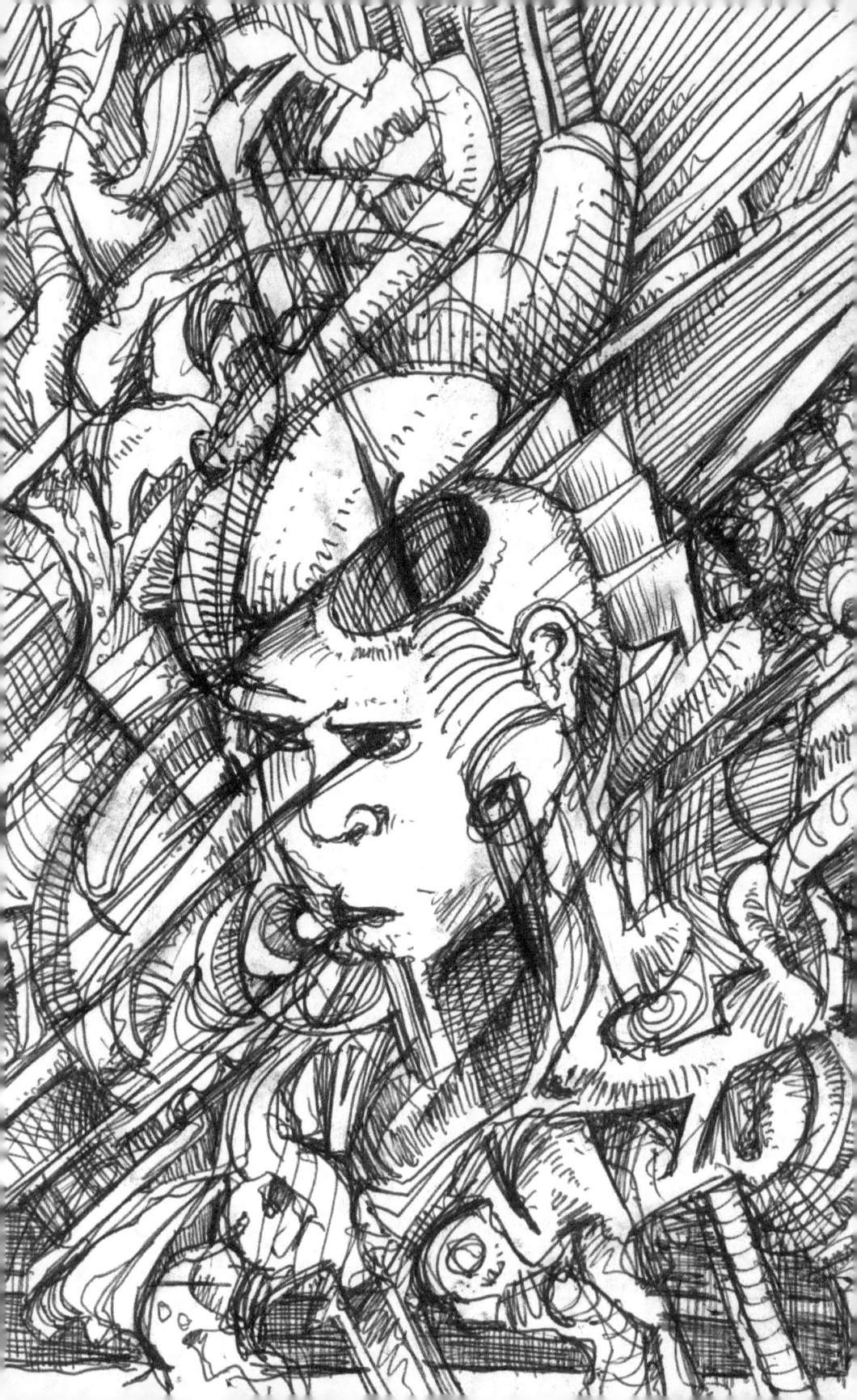

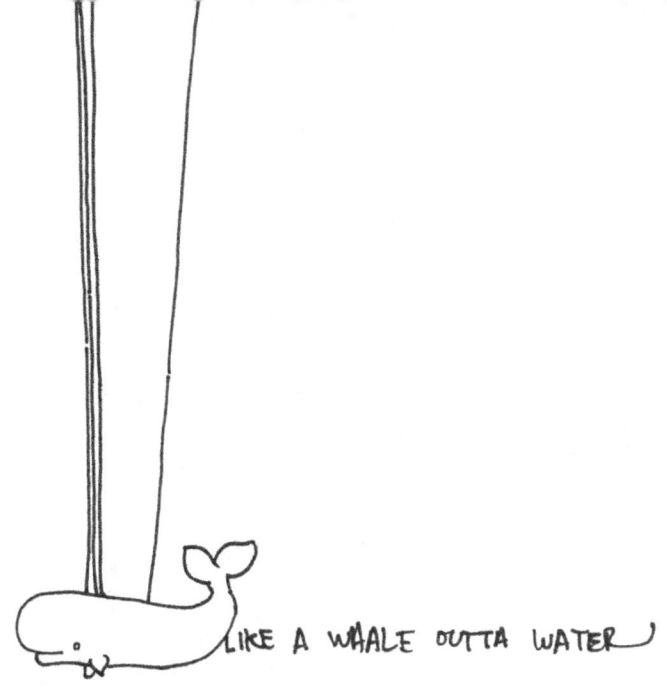

LIKE A WHALE OUTTA WATER

WHY HELLO MRS. NINE FANCY MEETING YOU HERE
WHAT BRINGS YOU AROUND THESE PARTS AT
THIS TIME OF NIGHT WITH THAT CROWN ON YOUR
HEAD AND THOSE MOCCASINS ON YOUR TOES
LIKE SOME ROYAL BACKWOODS TOMATO READY
TO GET SALTY AND SLICED UP IN THE BACKYARD
WHERE THE CHRISTMAS LIGHTS ARE STRUNG
UP YEAR-ROUND AND JENNY JOHNNER'S ABOVE-
GROUND POOL PARTIES RAGE FOR HALF-HOURS
AT A TIME SCARING THE GROUNDHOGS DEEP
INTO THE EARTH TO WHILE AWAY THE EONS IN
RELATIVE COMFORT AND ADJUSTABLE LUMBAR
SUPPORT TO PREVENT LONG TERM LUMBAGO AND
POTASSIUM DEFICIENCY OF THE UPPER ELEMENTS
AND THROUGHOUT THE ENTIRE STRATOSPHERE UP
WHERE THE BIRDS FLY AND SWOOP WITH LITTLE
GOOGLY GOGGLES SLUNG LOW ON THEIR NECKS
TO HIDE THE BLISTERS FROM SOME MISPRESCRIBED
OINTMENTS OR BALMS TO SOOTHE THOSE POUNDING
HEADACHES WE ALL GET AFTER STUBBING A TOE OR
TWO ON YOUR EGO OR PILED UP DIRTY CLOTHES IN THE MIND.

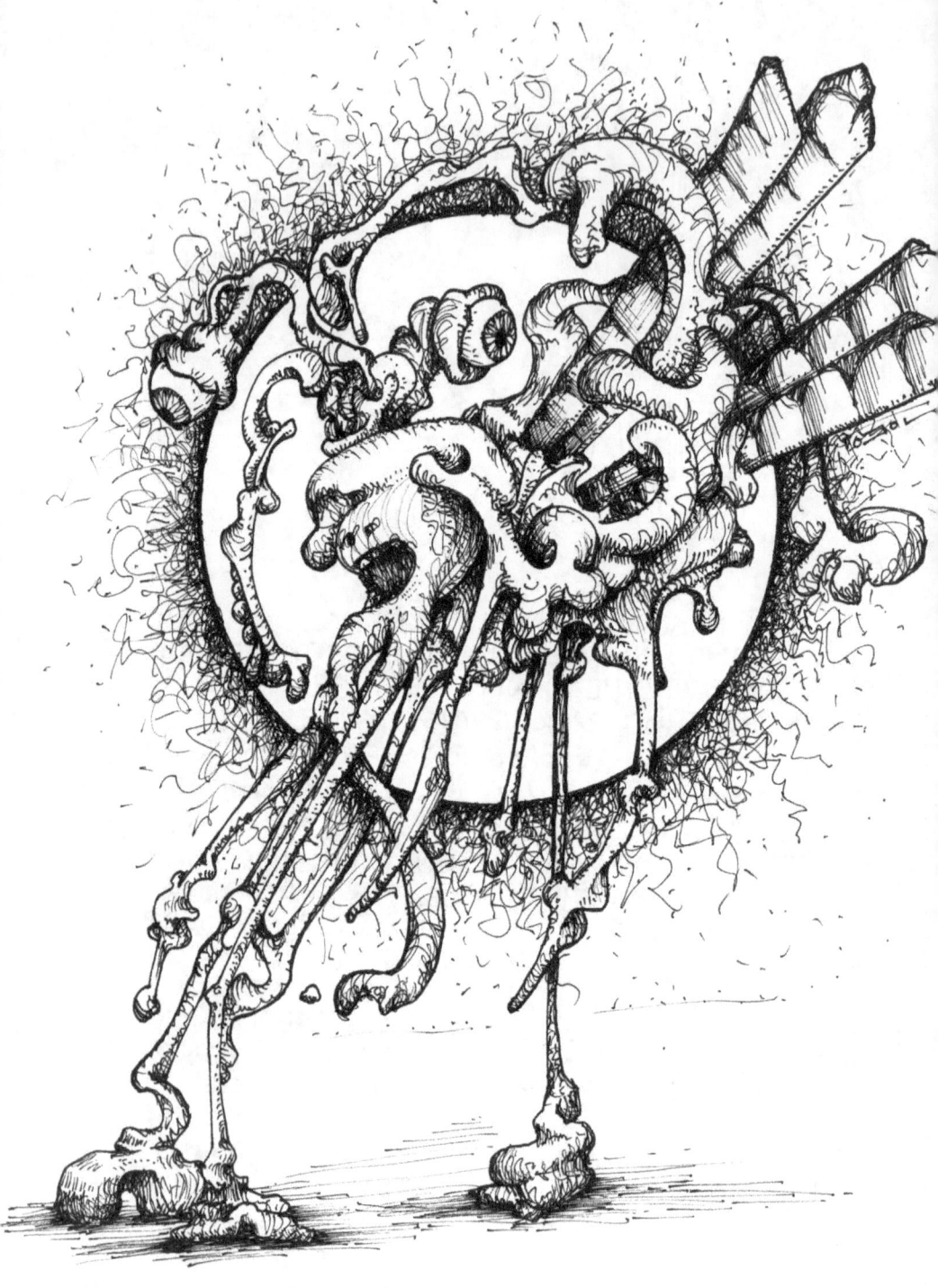

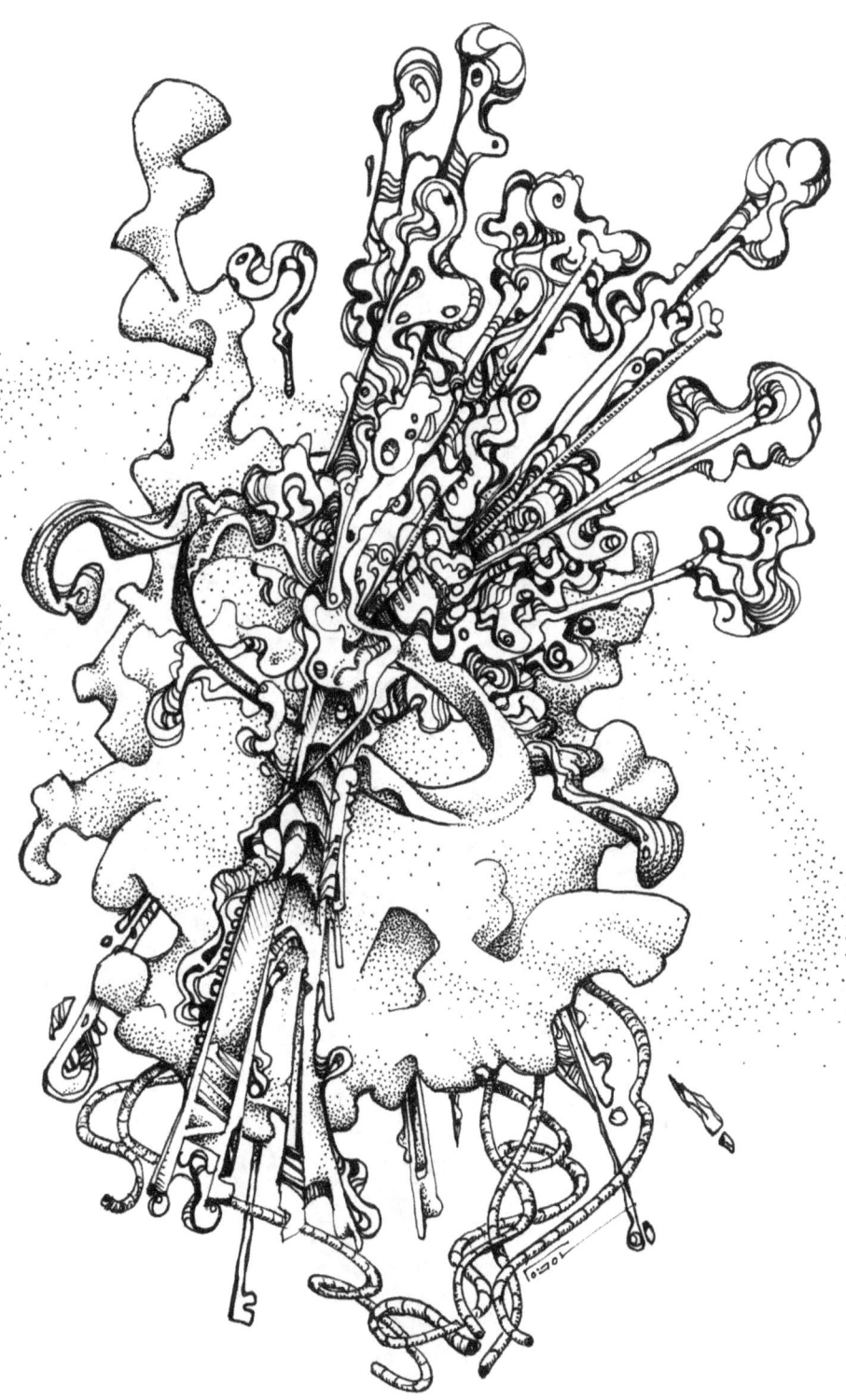

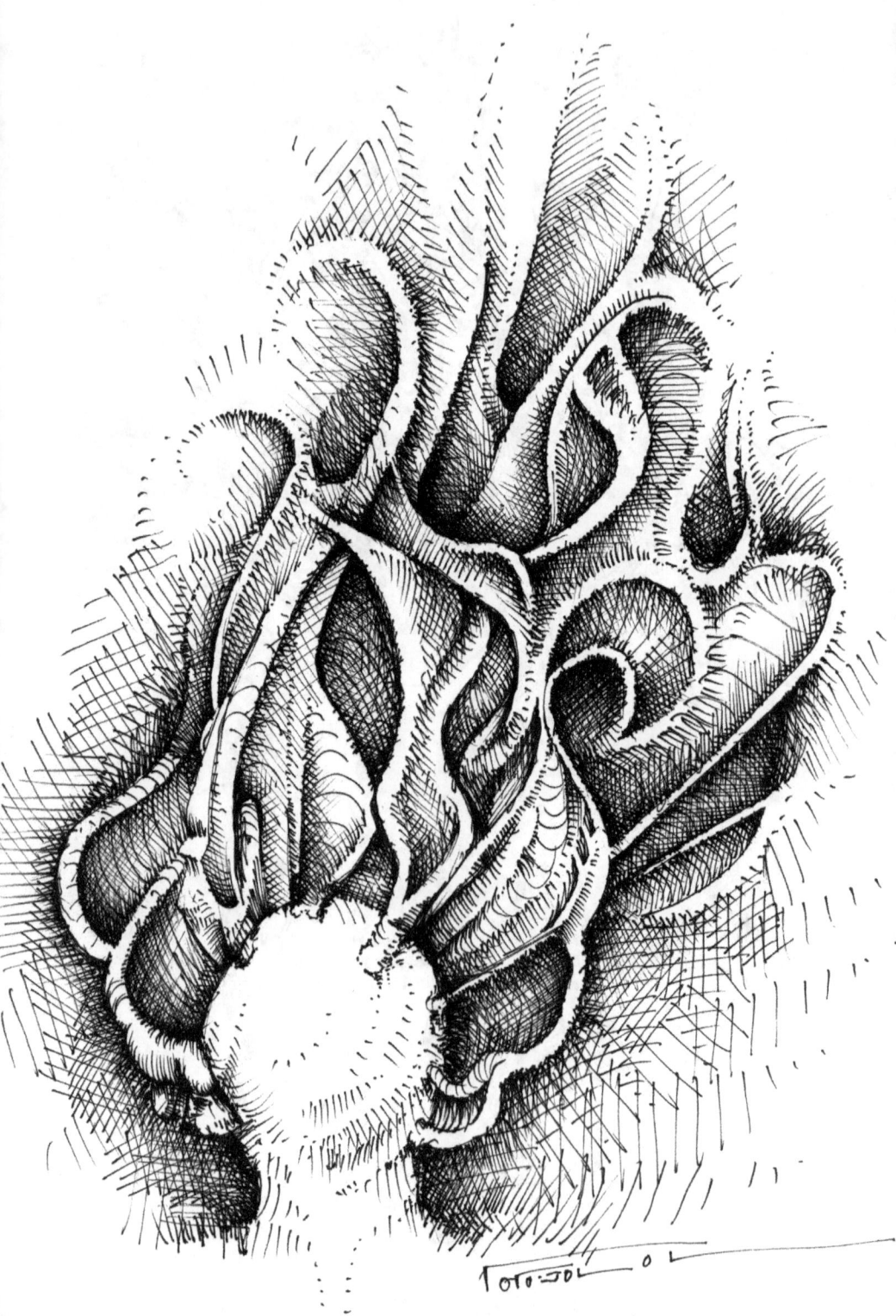

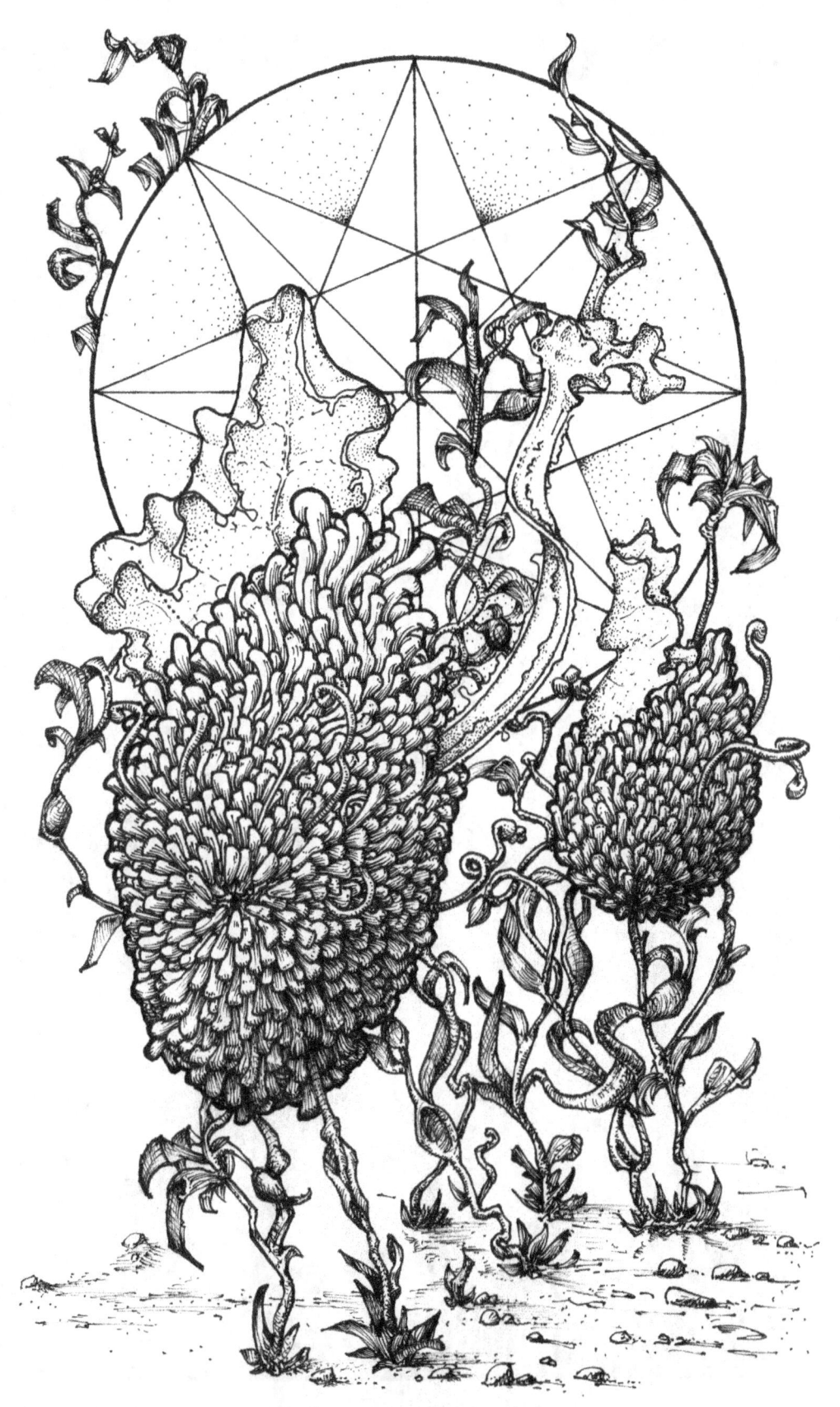

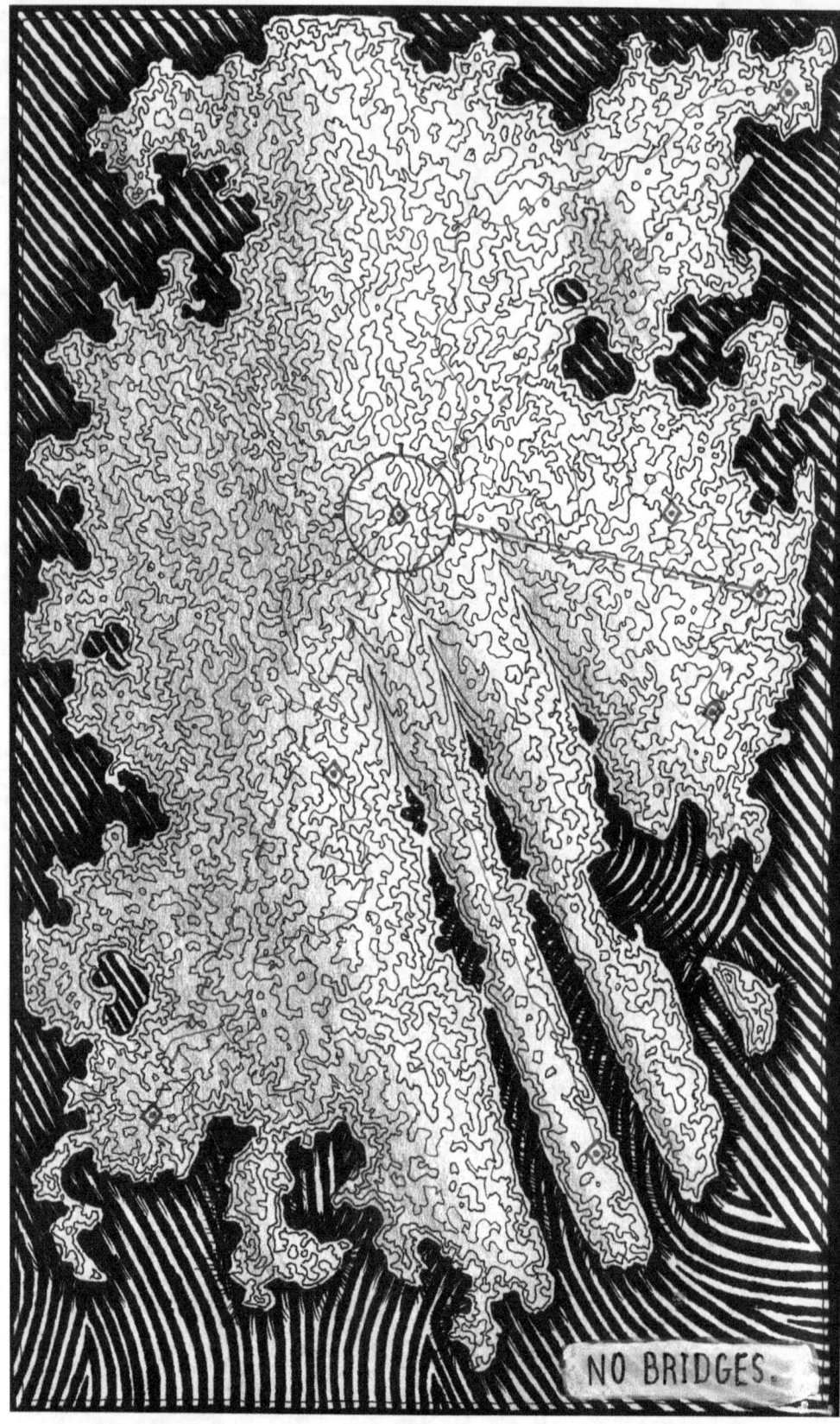

NO BRIDGES.

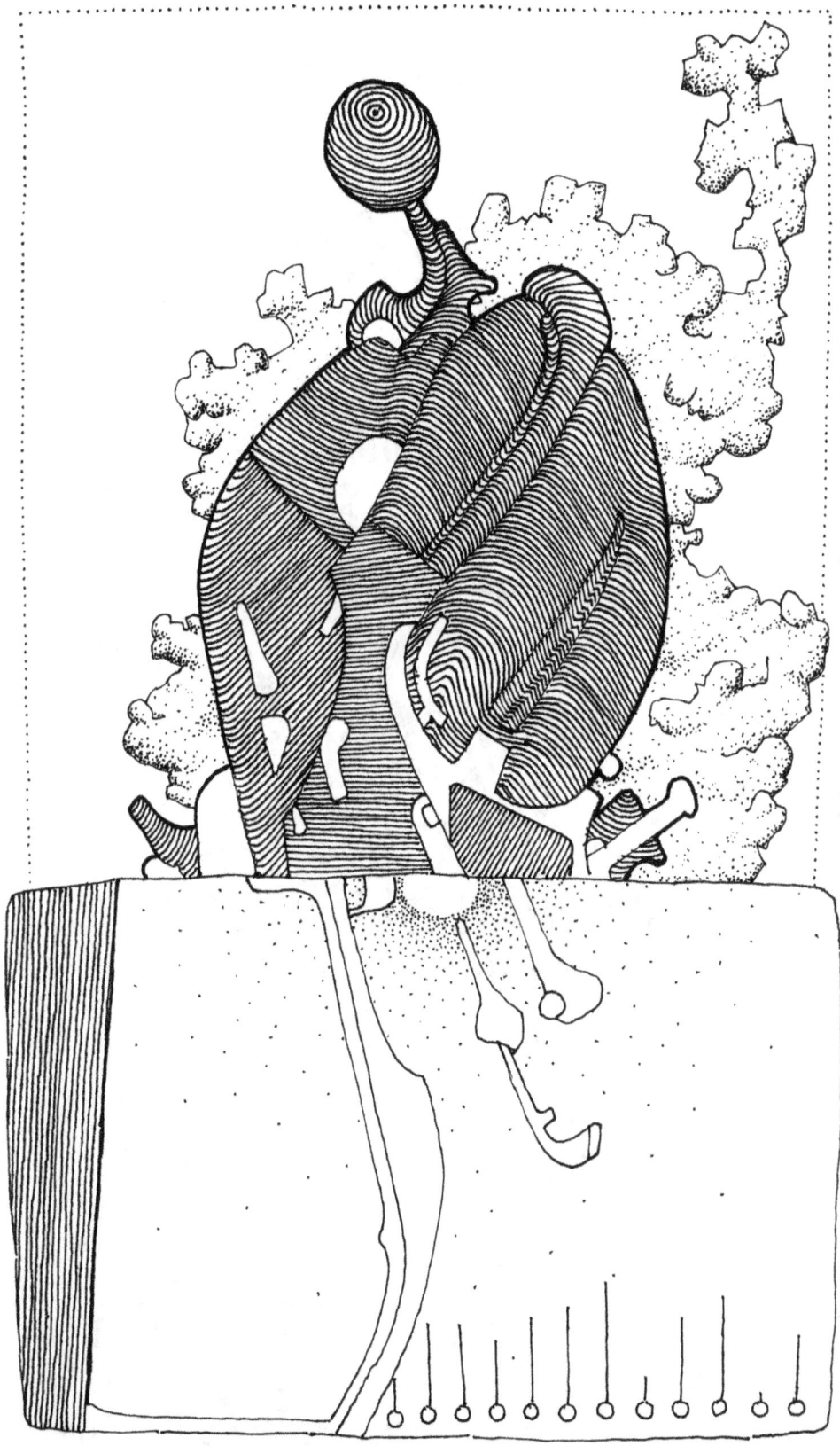

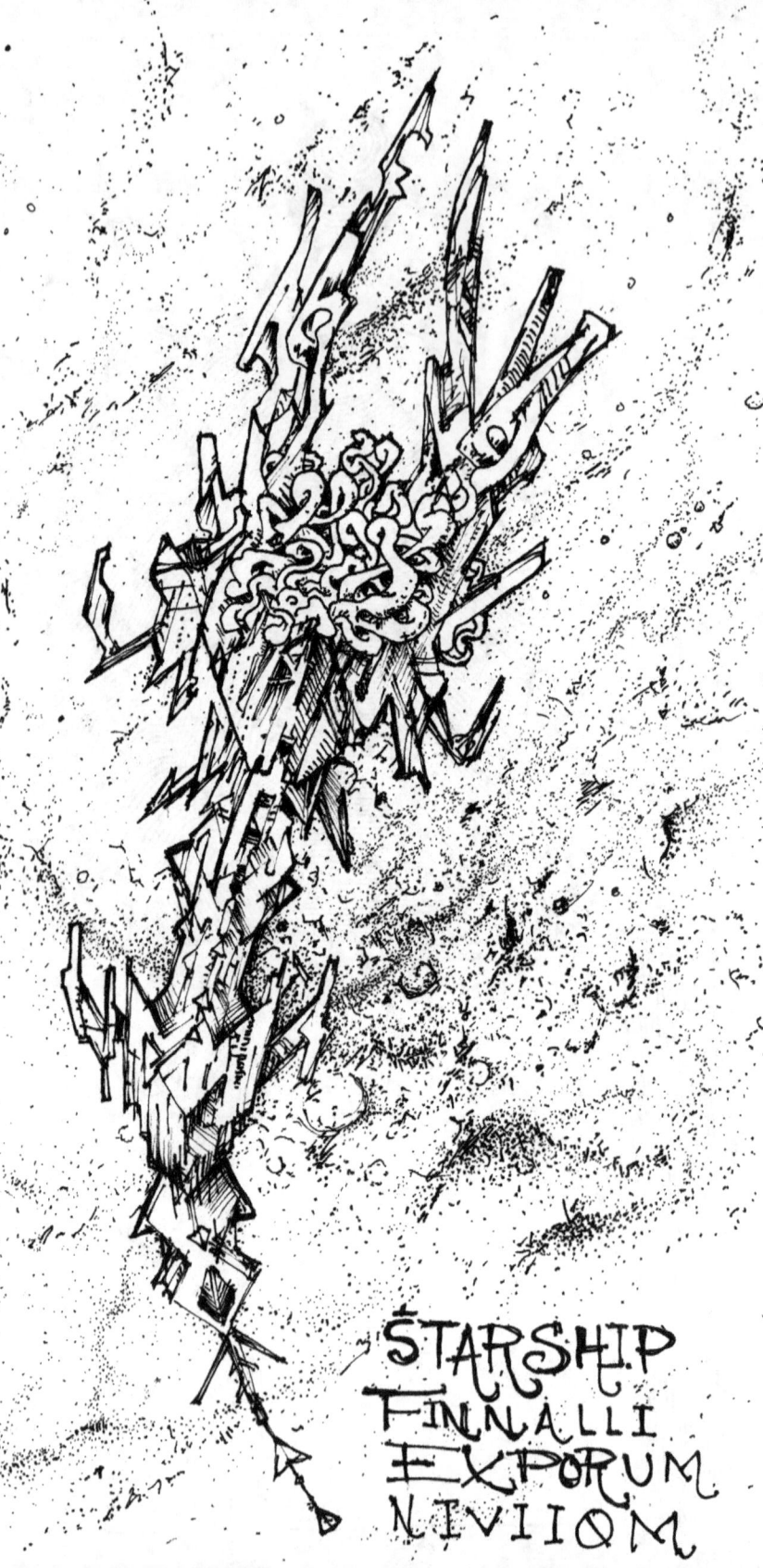

STARSHIP
FINNALLI
EXPORUM
NIVIIOM

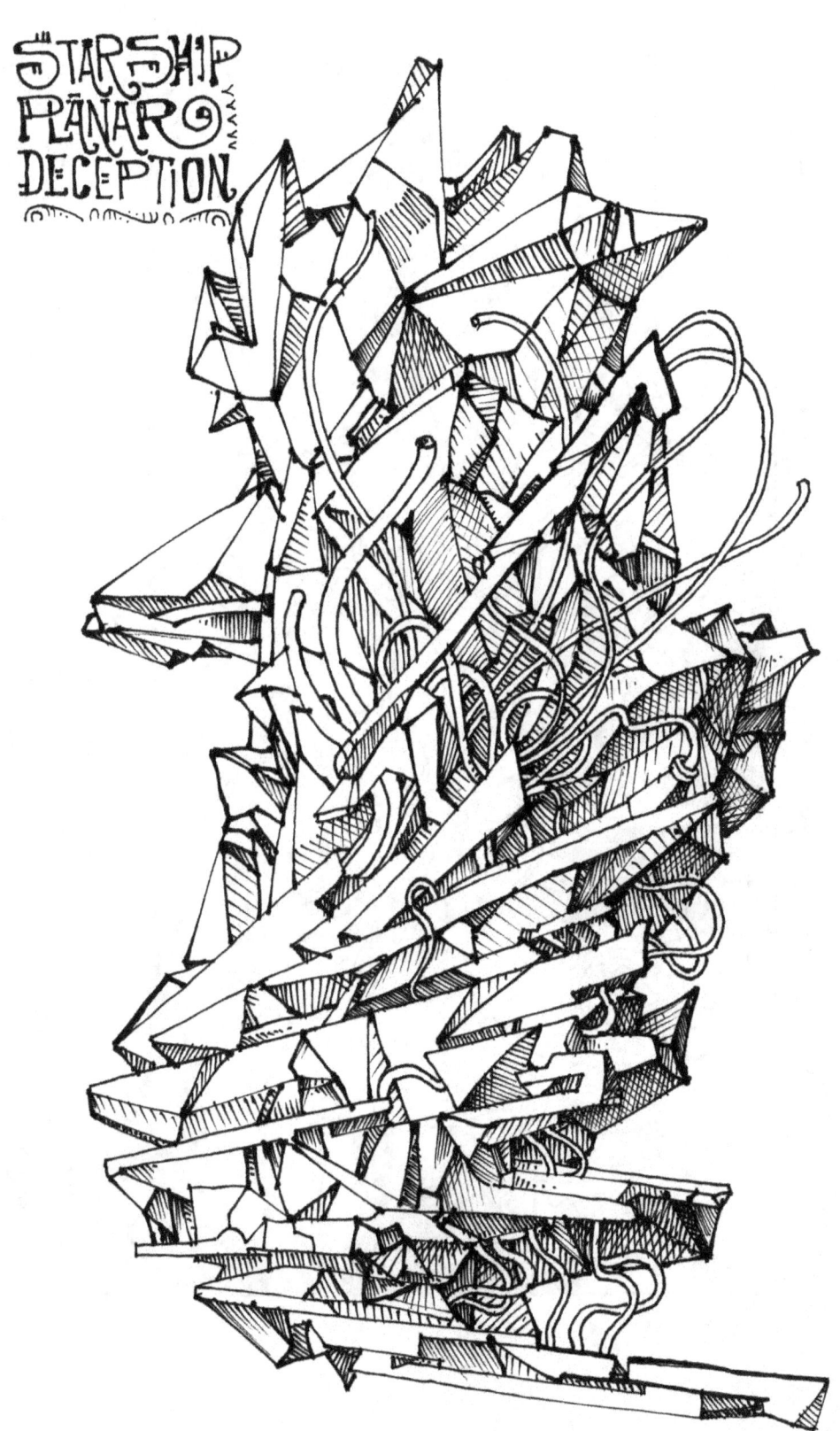

STARSHIP
PLANAR
DECEPTION

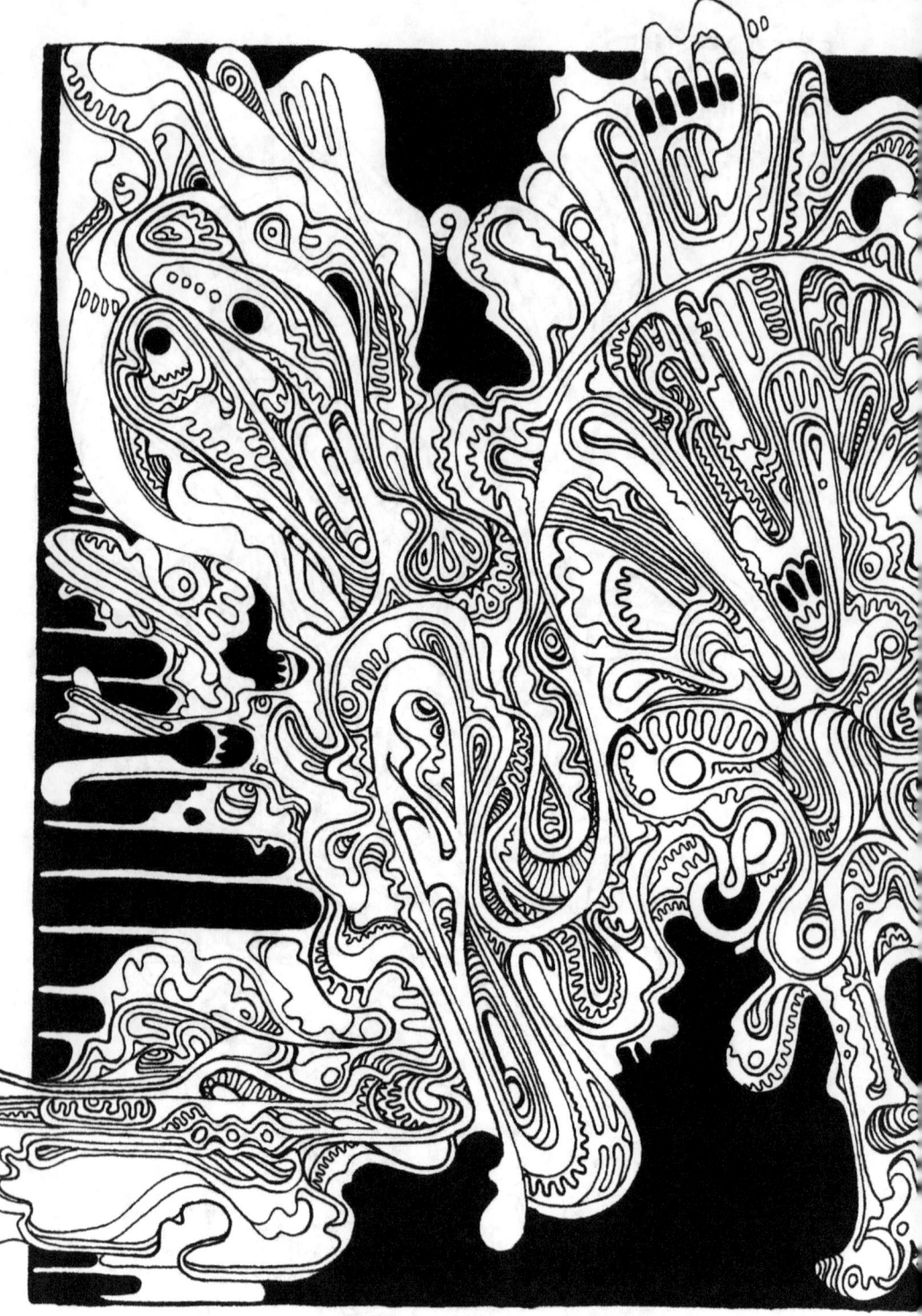

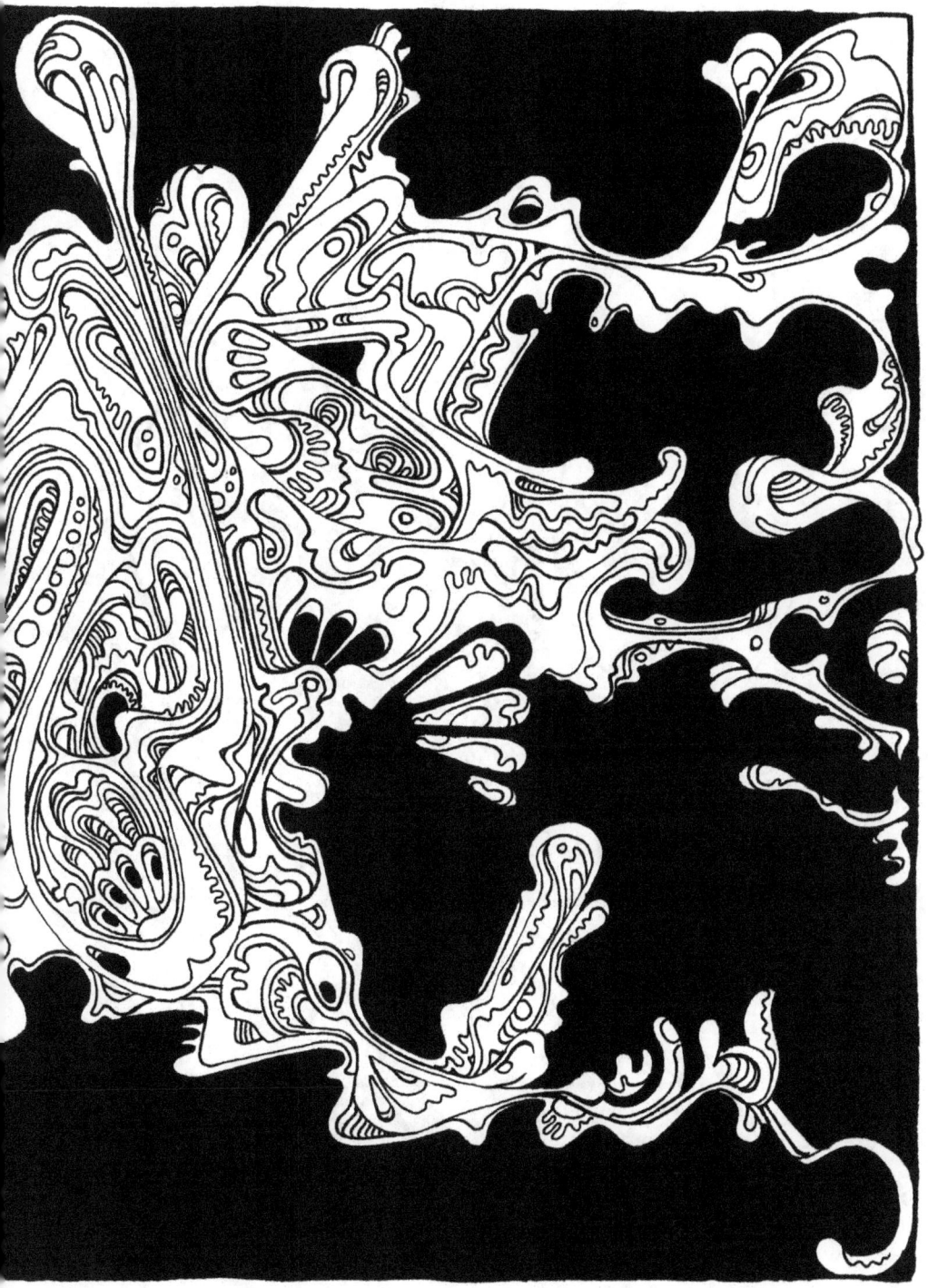

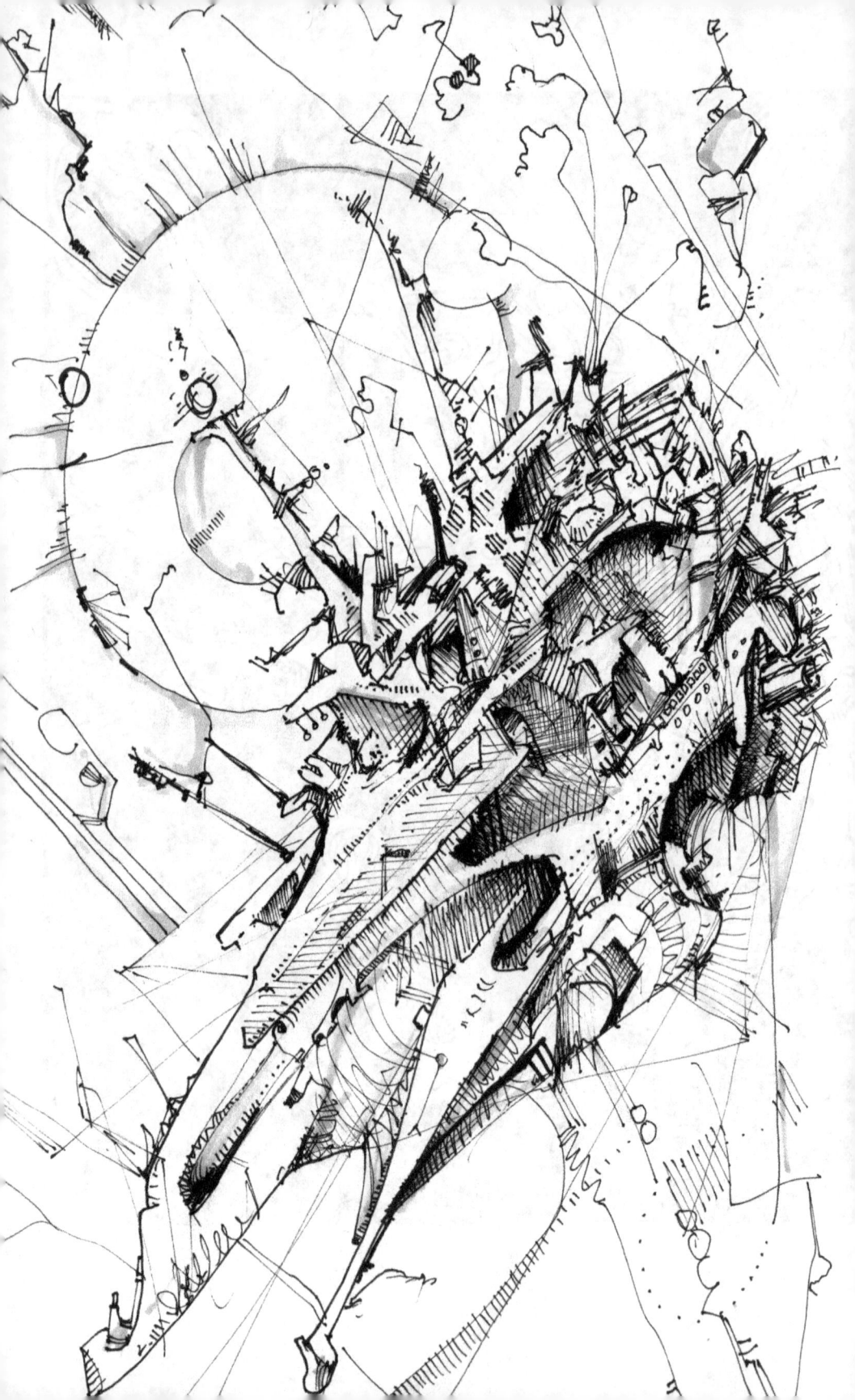

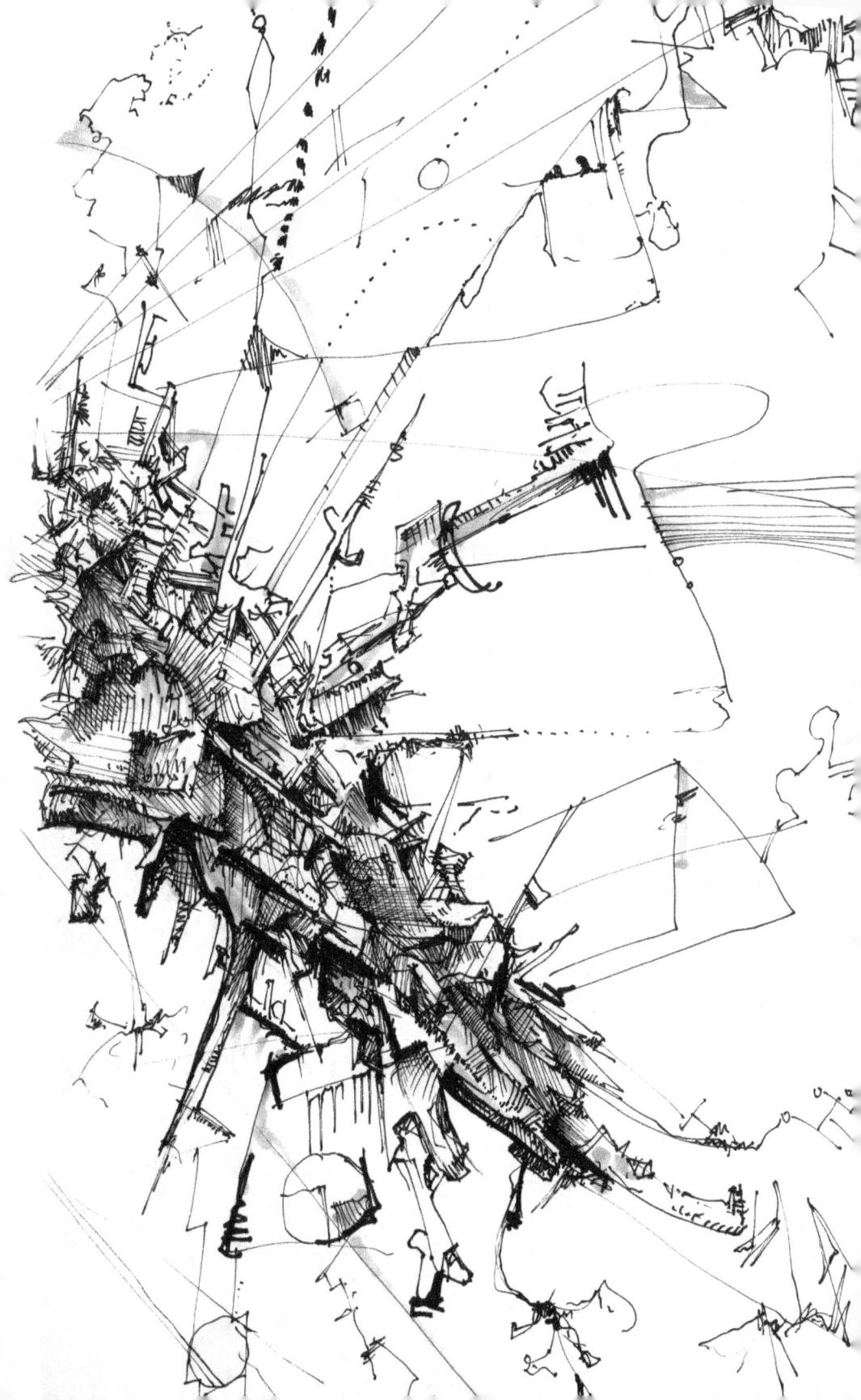

PLEASE BEHOLD NOW THE DRAWER
HOLDING KNICK-KNACKS GALORE
HE FLEW OUT OF THE DESK
AND ACROSS THE FLOOR

"ENOUGH!" AND HE SWORE
AS HE EMPTIED MID SOAR
AN OATH VIKING-ESQUE
"BY THE HAMMER OF THOR!"

CREATING A MESS TOO BIG
TO IGNORE
HE LANDED AND SKIDDED
ACROSS TO THE DOOR
AND HE SIGHED AND WHISPERED
AND SLOWLY CONFESSED
HE JUST DIDN'T WANT TO BE
A DRAWER ANYMORE.

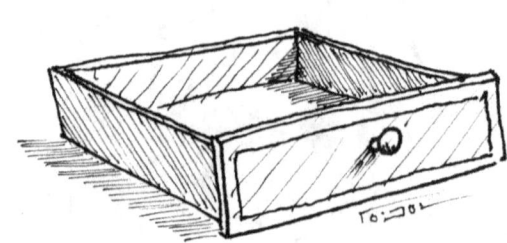

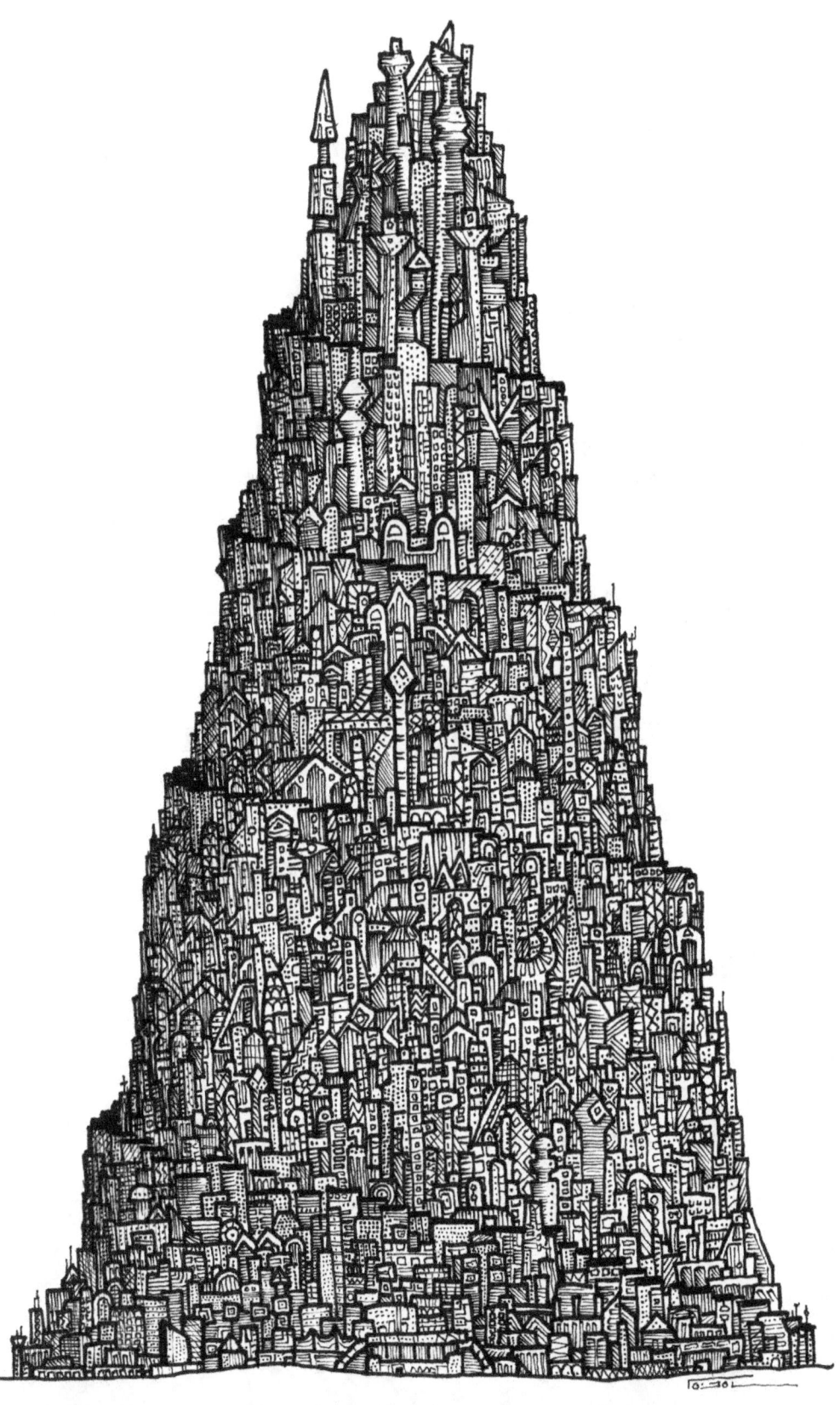

FAT

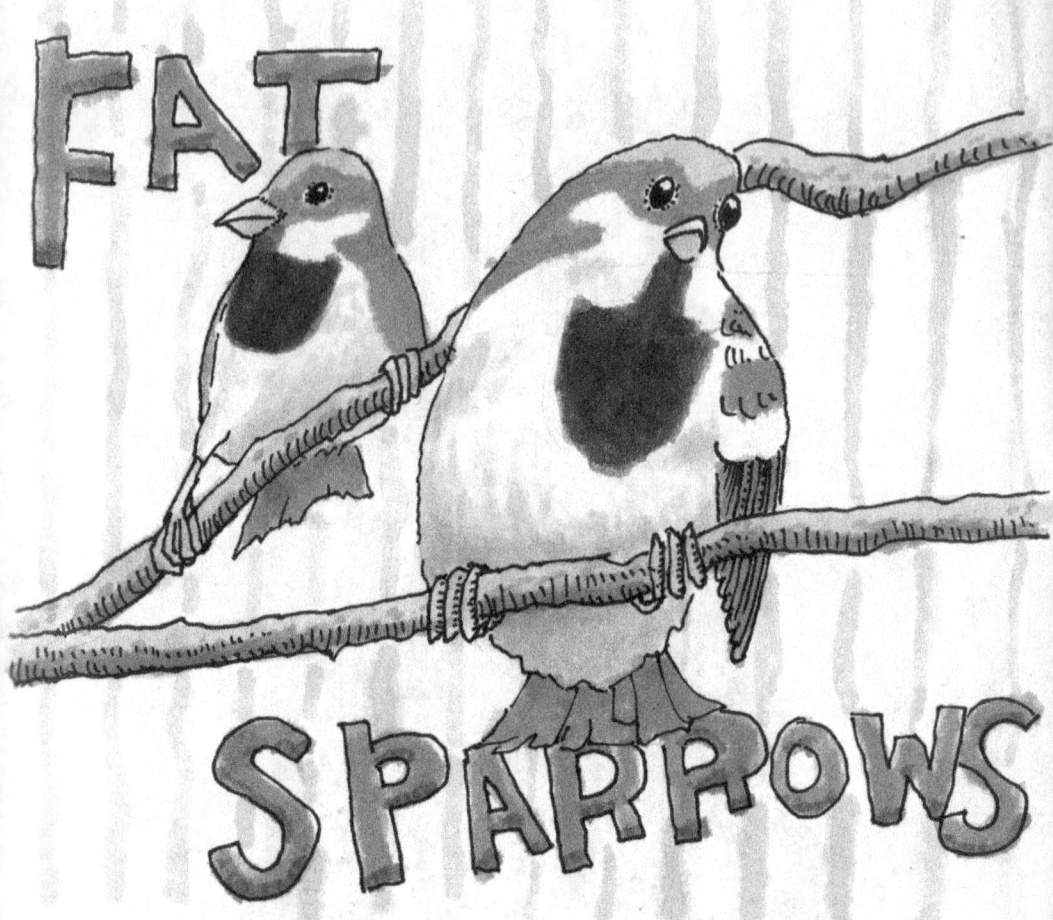

SPARROWS

TWO FAT SPARROWS ON A BOUGH
ONE FOR LOOKOUT, ONE FOR SPYING,
SEARCHING FOR ONE SLUGGISH COW
THEY COULD CATCH BY LABORED FLYING.

AND NOW DESCENDING WINGS AFLUTTER
UPON A BOVINE THEY'D BEEN EYEING,
THEY ATE IT ALL EXCEPT THE UDDER,
AND WENT ON LIVING BY ITS DYING.

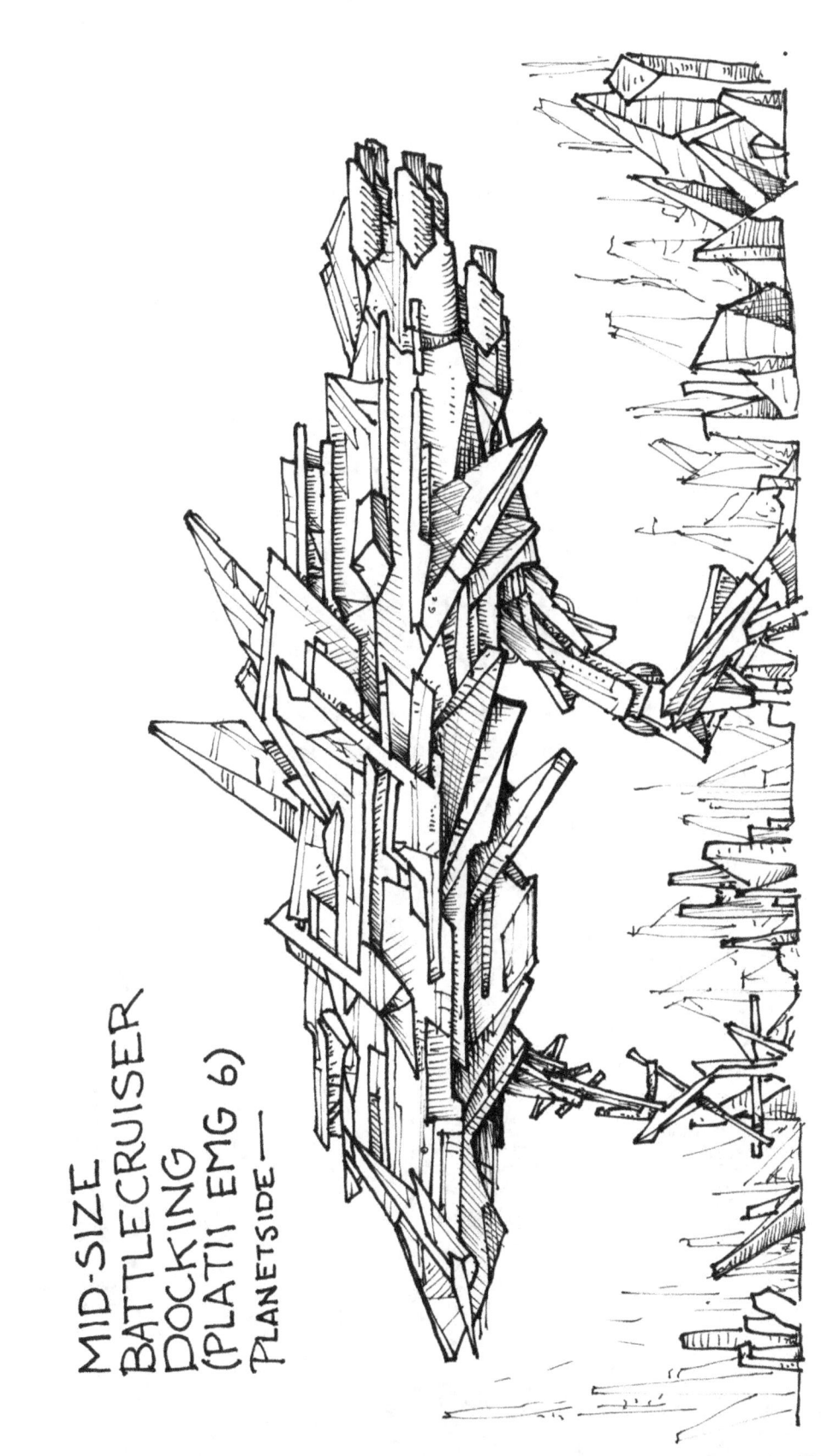

MID-SIZE
BATTLECRUISER
DOCKING
(PLATⅡ EMG 6)
—PLANETSIDE—

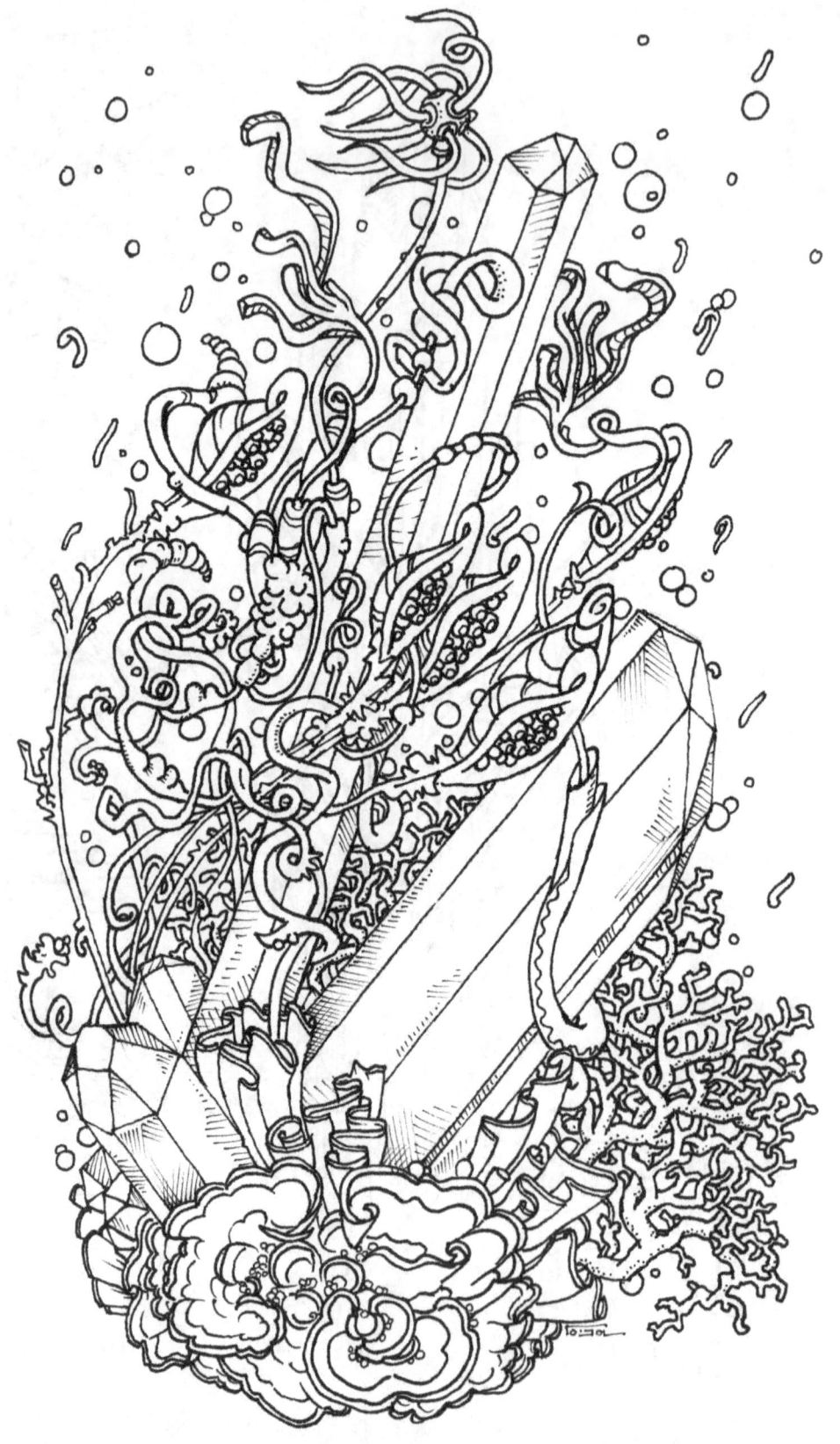

There was a lump that inched along,
  it inched along all day.
And as it crawled it hummed a song;
  its song and skin were oh so grey.
I tried to ask it what was wrong,
  but it could never say.
It had no mouth, it had no lungs,
  and so I walked ~~along~~ away.

So long it crawled,
  so long it tried,
  to reach its destination.
Its song it drawled,
  Its heart, it sighed,
  there was no consolation.

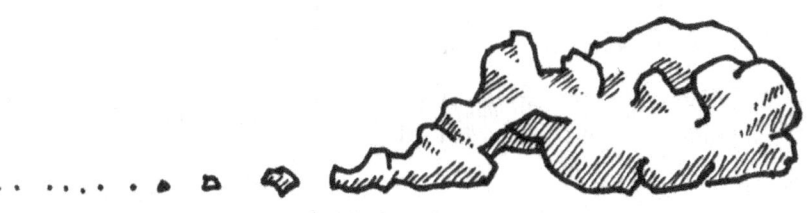

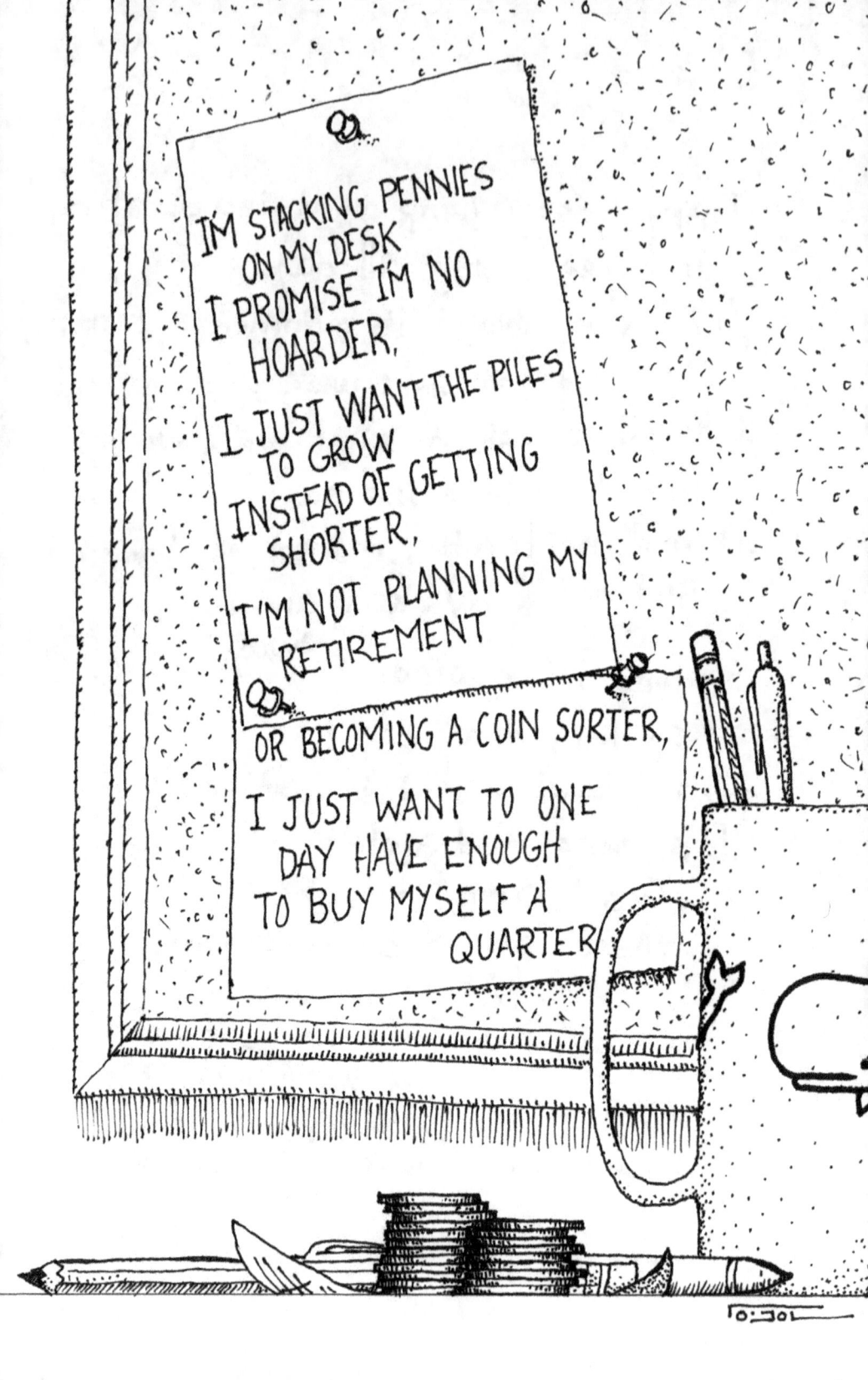

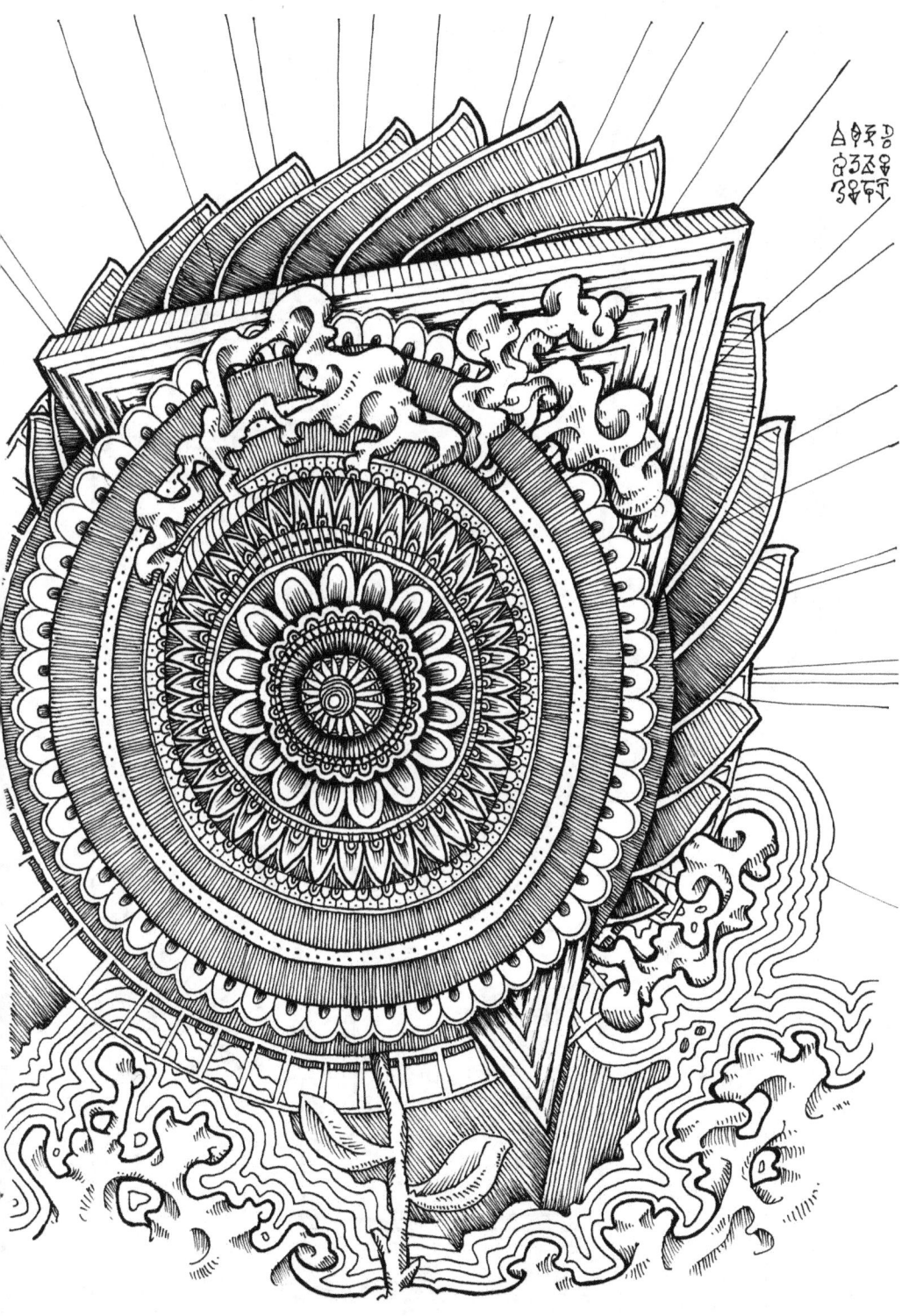

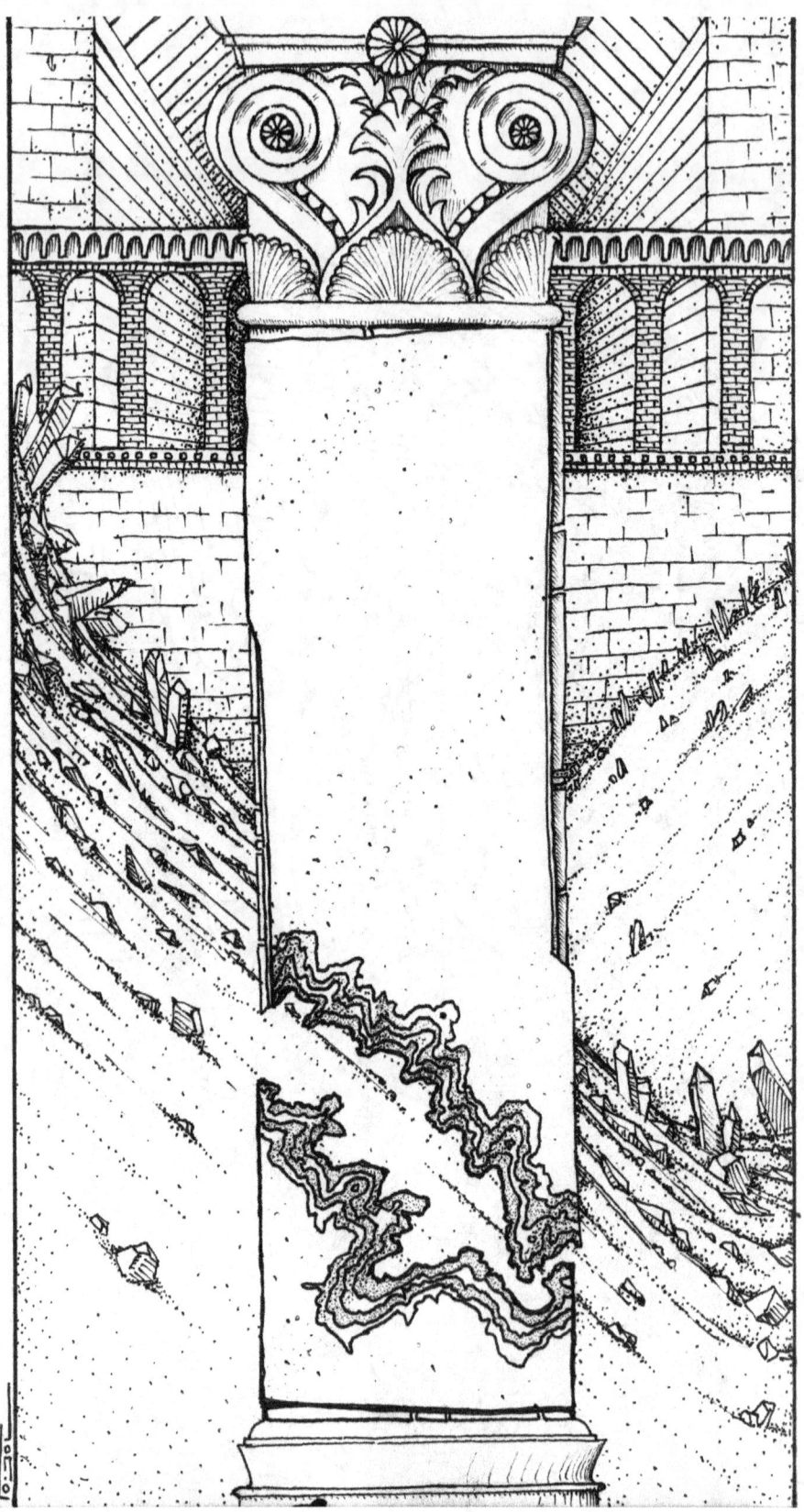

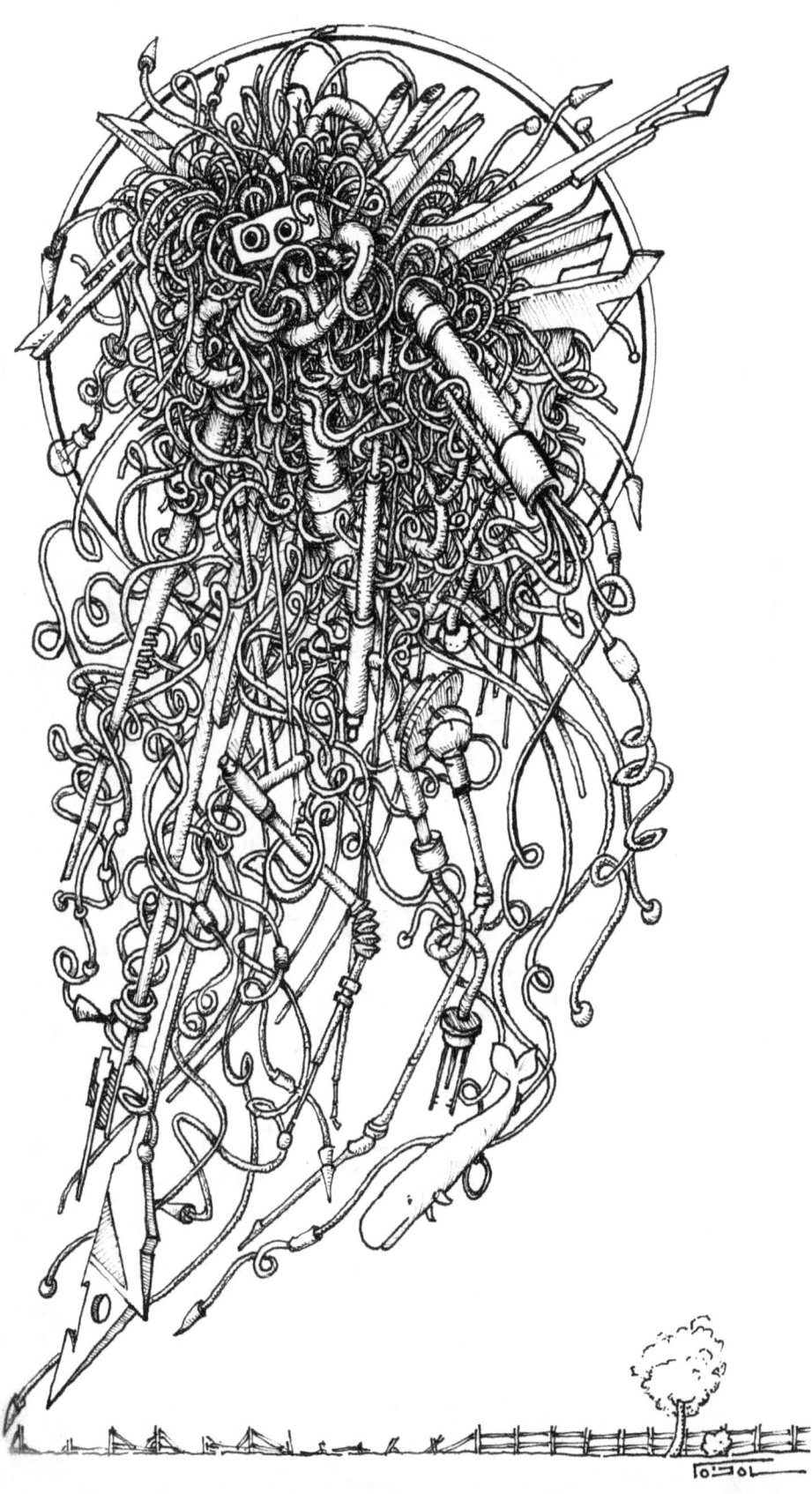

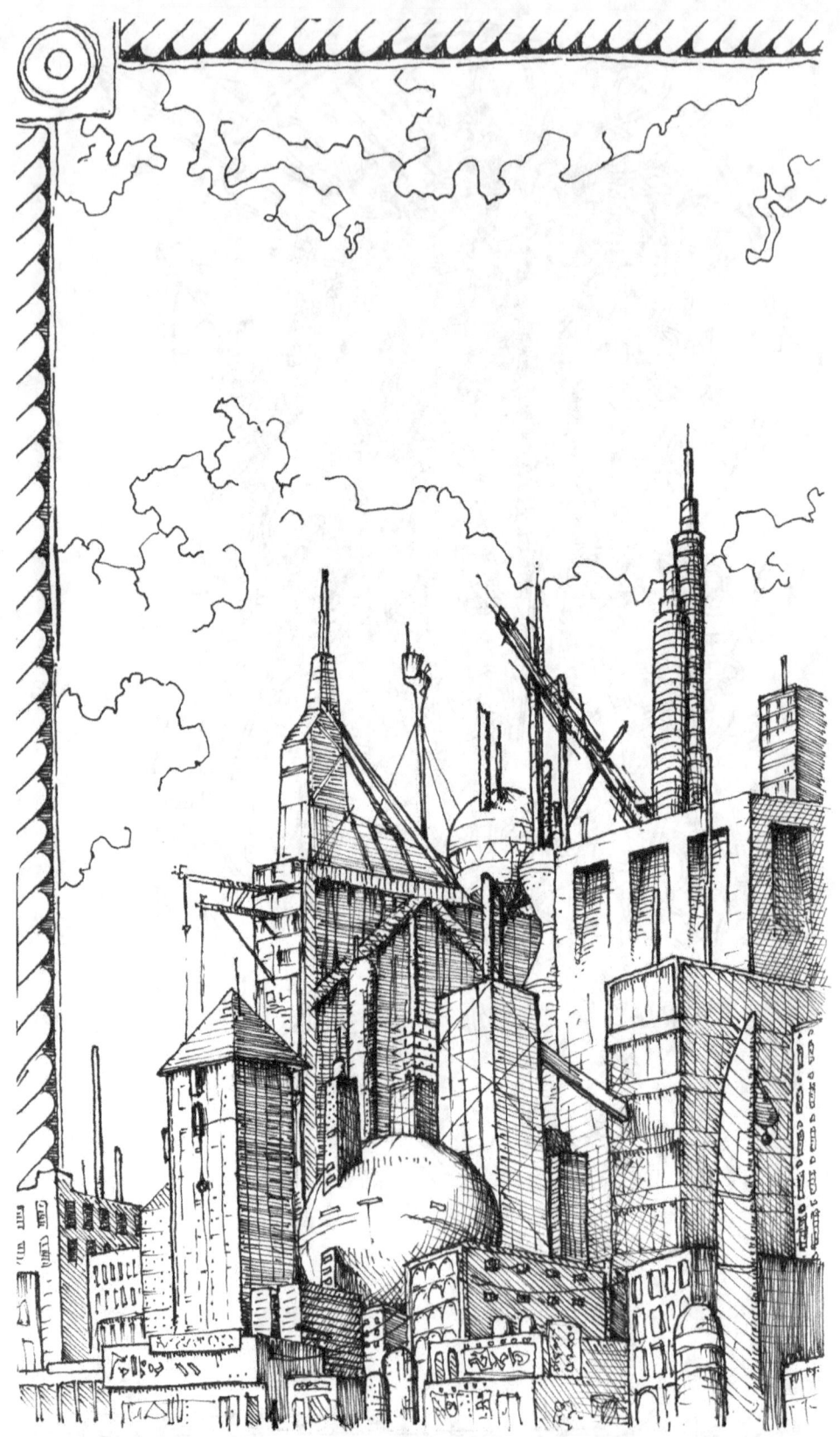

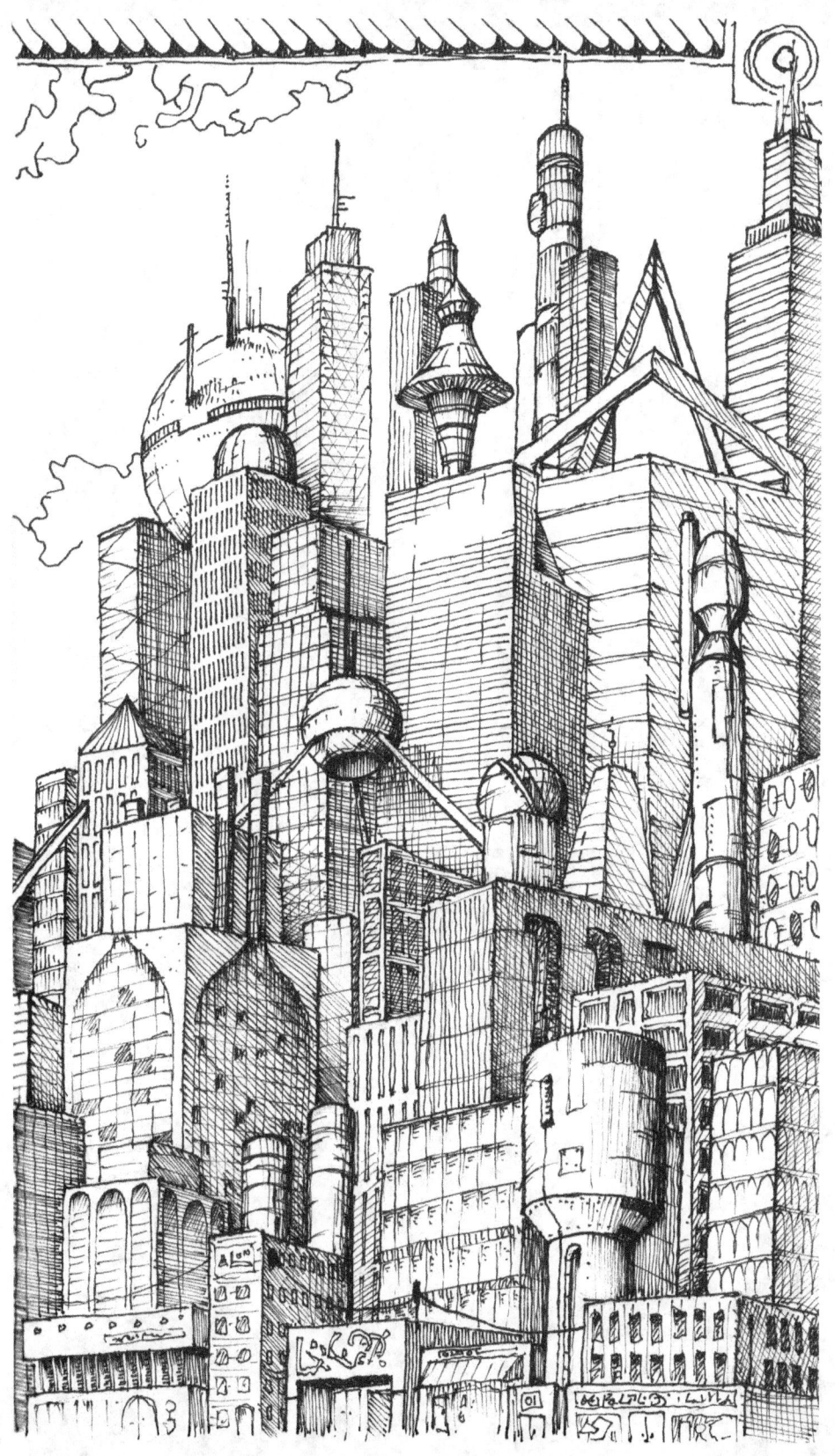

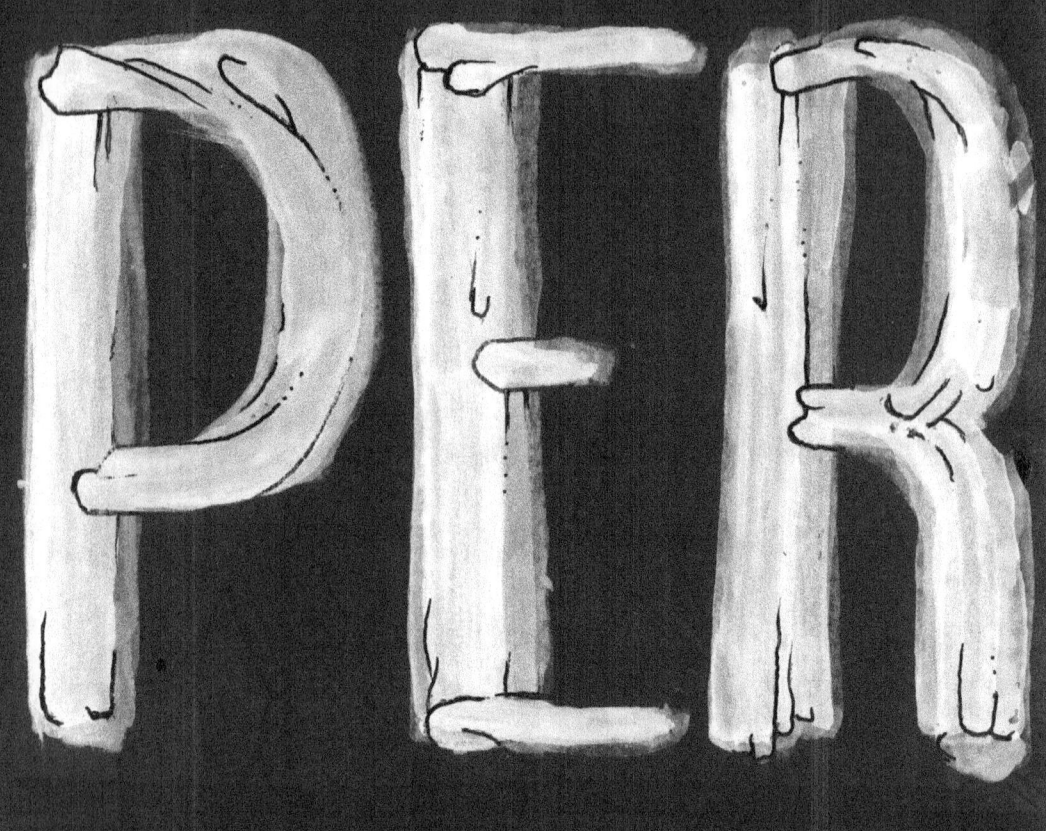

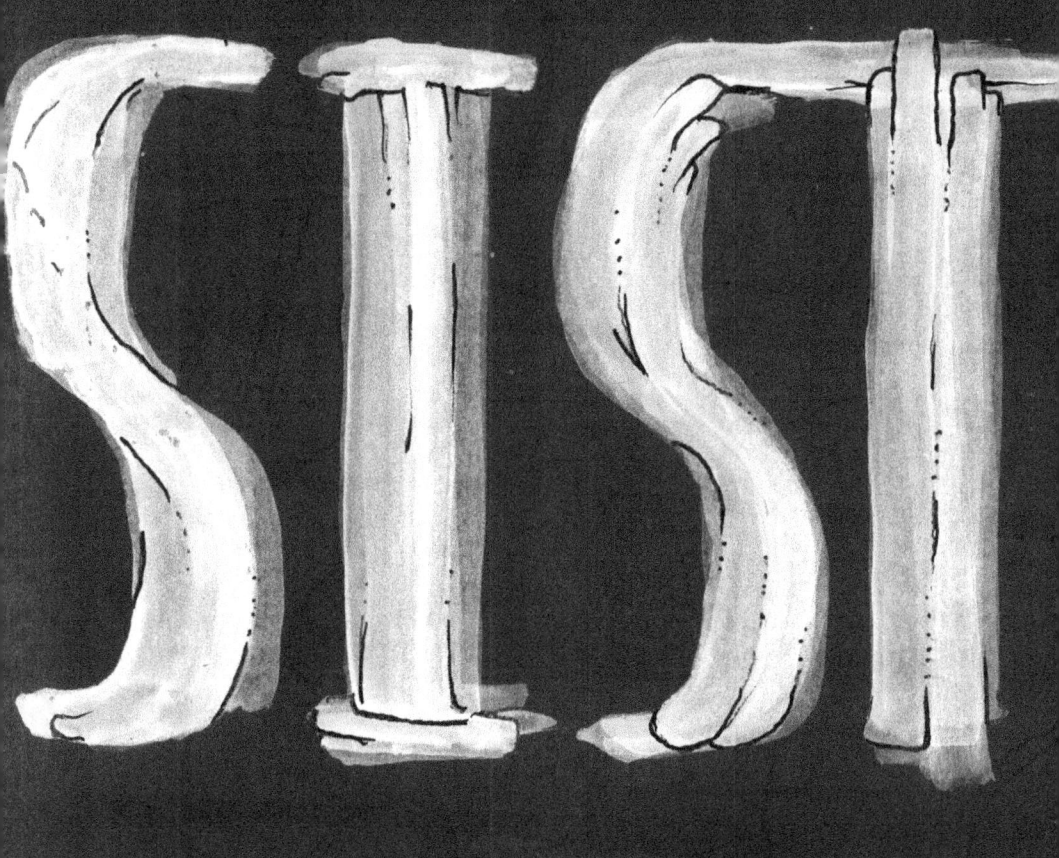

www.ingramcontent.com/pod-product-compliance
Lightning Source LLC
Chambersburg PA
CBHW070326190526
45169CB00005B/1768